Nuclear Apartheid: Bullying, Hypocrisy and the Double Standards on Nuclear Weapons

SAGHIR IQBAL

ISBN-10: 1983910414
ISBN-13: 978-1983910418

DEDICATION

I dedicate this book to all those who gave me encouragement, support and guidance. Foremost, to my father (late) Raja Mohammed Iqbal and to my mother Azra Begum, from whom I have learnt so much. In addition to my wife Neghat Khan, who was patient and extremely helpful in my trying times. And finally I dedicate this to Raja Shahid Ahmed, Raja Jahangir Khan, Raja Mohammed Yasin (Diamond), Raja Nadir Yasin and Raja Mohammed Naheem Khan.

CONTENTS

ACKNOWLEDGMENTS

I am very grateful to a host of people for their various contributions towards this book. I am particularly very grateful to Professor Syed Peerzada Mahmud Shah Bookhari who deserves much commendation for his constant encouragement and support throughout the hard times of the programme. In addition, I am also very grateful to Noreen Shah, Noreen Akhtar, Shaheen Hussain and Husnaa Tahir for their constant support.

Nuclear Apartheid: Bullying, Hypocrisy and the Double Standards on Nuclear Weapons

Image/pixabay.com/atomic bomb test

Abstract

This book looks at the proliferation of weapons of mass destruction and the double standards and hypocrisy practiced by the five declared nuclear powers. It gives a brief short history of nuclear development in the declared nuclear countries and the impact of nuclear war. It argues that the only way to eradicate these horrendous weapons is for the five declared nuclear powers to make immediate measures to dismantle the weapons and stockpiles of weaponised materials – as they had agreed under the Nuclear Non-Proliferation Treaty (NPT).

Over 2 billion people could be affected by a nuclear exchange in a conflict between India and Pakistan from only 50 nuclear bombs. Research had indicated this could have a tremendous effect on the environment and on food security. The potential for a nuclear conflict across other regions of the globe is high - such as North Korea, Iran and Israel.

Nuclear artillery test

Abbreviation

AG - Australia Group

ALCM/GLCM – Air Launched Cruise Missile/ Ground Launched Cruise
Missile

CTBT - Comprehensive Test Ban Treaty

FMCT - Fissile Material Cut off Treaty

HEU -   Highly-enriched Uranium

IAEA - International Atomic Energy Agency

NAS - Nuclear-armed States

NCA - National Command Authority

NNWS - Non-Nuclear Weapon States

NPT - Nuclear Non-proliferation Treaty

NSG - Nuclear Suppliers Group

NWFZ - Nuclear Weapons Free Zones

NWS - Nuclear Weapons States

MTCR - Missile Technology Control Regime

NATO - North Atlantic Treaty Organisation

PGM - Precision guided munitions (Smart weapons)

SAFARI-I - South African Fundamental Atomic Research Installation

UAV – Unmanned Aerial Vehicle

UK - United Kingdom

UN - United Nations

UNSC - United Nations Security Council

USA - United States of America

WMD - Weapons of Mass Destruction

WA - Wassenaar Arrangements

ZC - Zangger Committee

1 INTRODUCTION TO NUCLEAR SECURITY

Image/pixabay.com/nuclear capable submarine

The global security challenges since World War II and thereafter (post-Cold war period) has affected many countries. This has resulted in a number of countries pursuing a nuclear weapons programme to provide them with the ultimate security – the belief that the fear of utter annihilation of their opponents would result in deterrence and eventually detente. According to Kristensen and Norris (2014), there are approximately 16,300 nuclear weapons located at some 97 sites in 14 countries. Many of these weapons are in military arsenals (roughly 10,000), with the remaining ones being in the process of retirement and awaiting dismantlement.

They state that 93% of the total global inventory resides in Russia and the United States of America (USA). The remaining weapon stockpiles are in the United Kingdom (UK), France, China, Israel, India, Pakistan and North Korea. In addition, 180 USA nuclear bombs are stored in the five non-nuclear NATO allies (Belgium, Germany, Italy, the Netherlands, and Turkey). These weapons have been developed for a number of reasons such as security, great power status, maintaining regional or global hegemony. The risks of an inadvertent conflict are high and could lead to a nuclear exchange that would be catastrophic in regards to the loss of life and the negative impact on the environment.

There is a two tier system in regards to nuclear weapons development – the haves and the have-nots. This has led to a system of nuclear apartheid, where a self-selected few are dominating the rest of the world in nuclear weapons capability. USA, Russia, China, France and the United Kingdom are the five declared nuclear powers who continue to keep the monopoly in this area. They have devised an NPT treaty (Nuclear Non-proliferation Treaty) for the rest of the world to sign in which they will not purse or develop nuclear weapons; they will however be able to share in civilian nuclear technology (Davis, 2009).

The former head of the International Atomic Energy Agency (IAEA), Mohamed El Baradei, described this two tier system as unworkable. He stated, "the way of thinking that it is morally reprehensible for some countries to pursue weapons of mass destruction yet morally acceptable for others to rely on them for security and indeed to continue to refine their capacities and postulate plans for their use" (Singh.2010). He argued that this two tier system would be difficult to work due to its discriminatory tendencies.

Hence, despite the NPT treaty a few countries had gate crashed the system and pursued their own weapons – India, Israel, Pakistan, South Africa and North Korea. This has resulted in other countries such as Iran to pursue nuclear weapons for their own security. With a number of countries pursuing nuclear weapons, there is a genuine fear of the proliferation of weapons of mass destructions (nuclear), which could eventually annihilate millions of people across the world (Davis, 2009).

The purpose of this book is to assess the double standards on nuclear weapons in the developing world that the five declared nuclear powers have all adhere to – Neo-nuclear apartheid. It will look at the dilemma faced by humanity and the ways to end this neo-nuclear apartheid and the abolition of these terrible weapons of mass destruction (Gusterson, 2006).

For instance, to fully understand the nuclear behaviour of states such as Pakistan, the Indian case must be considered. India's nuclear programme was due to a number of reasons such as, global status and regional hegemonic designs on the one hand and security parameters on the other – this changed Pakistan's behaviour towards global non-proliferation. Pakistan's nuclear programme cannot be dealt with separately from that of India. To regulate Pakistan's behaviour it is necessary to change India's behaviour, to change India's behaviour there is a need to change the behaviour of the Nuclear Weapons States (NWS) overall.

This is why the findings of this book contends that it is only a change in the behaviour of states at the global level that can lead to a change in the behaviour of states at a regional level. Hence, the double standards and hypocrisy needs to be eradicated from the five declared nuclear weapons states.

A Trident missile launched from a Royal Navy *Vanguard* class ballistic missile submarine

2 BRIEF NUCLEAR HISTORY

Image/pixabay.com/nuclear test

A total of nine countries have tested a nuclear device, with a number of other countries attempting to develop the nuclear bomb. The following five countries are seen as 'nuclear weapon states' under the Non-Proliferation Treaty (NPT): United States of America, Russia, United Kingdom, France and China.

India, Pakistan and North Korea (initially had signed the treaty but withdrew in 2003) are three countries that have also detonated a nuclear device but had not signed the NPT treaty. South Africa was another country that had successfully tested a nuclear device but later decided to voluntarily to dismantle its nuclear bombs and thereafter sign the NPT treaty.

The Countries of Belarus, Kazakhstan and the Ukraine had also relinquished the nuclear weapons on their territory since the demise of the former Soviet Union. In addition, it is thought that Israel has also developed nuclear weapons but chooses a policy of deliberate ambiguity in regards to this.

According to Kristensen and Norris (2014), there are approximately 16,300
nuclear weapons located at some 97 sites in 14 countries. These countries
that possess nuclear weapons are also known as members of the nuclear
club.

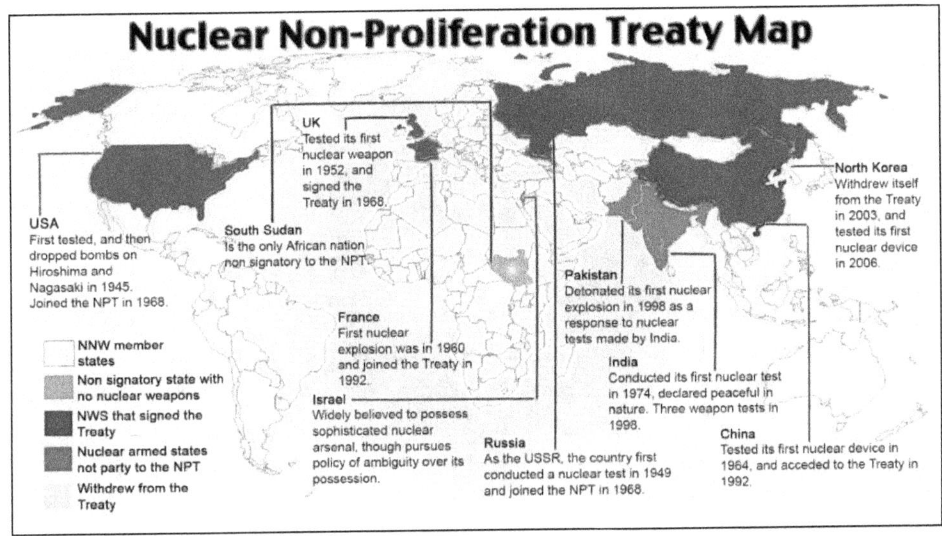

https://www.pressenza.com/2015/06/npt-consensus-failure-a-good-thing-108-countries-pledge-to-help-ban-nuclear-weapons/

NPT-designated nuclear weapon states	China, France, Russia, United Kingdom, United States
Non-NPT designated nuclear weapons states	India, Pakistan, North Korea
Suspected to have nuclear weapons	Israel

Nations hosting nuclear weapons **(NATO nuclear weapons sharing states**	NATO nuclear weapons sharing states - Belgium, Germany, Italy, Netherlands, Turkey
States formerly possessing nuclear weapons	Belarus, Kazakhstan, Ukraine, South Africa
Nations in nuclear alliances	Albania, Australia, Bulgaria, Canada, Croatia, Czech, Denmark, Estonia, Greece, Hungary, Iceland, Japan, Latvia, Lithuania, Luxembourg, Norway, Poland, Portugal, Romania, Slovakia, Slovenia, South Korea, Spain

There were an estimated 68,000 nuclear weapons in 1985 and due to a number of disarmament treaties the numbers had been reduced to 16,300 in 2014. It has been a huge reduction compared to 1985 estimates, but still the figure of 16,300 is a massive number in regards to active nuclear weapons. These weapons have the potential to cause catastrophic destruction across the globe. These five states are also the UN Security Council's permanent members with veto power.

Most of the declared nuclear powers have completed or are in the process of completing a TRIAD (three-sided military-force structure) system – in which nuclear weapons can be delivered by air, land and sea. The theory underlying the triad was that spreading the nuclear assets across various weapons platforms would make the nuclear arsenal more likely to survive an attack by an adversary and to be able to respond to a nuclear first strike successfully – giving some countries the ability for second-strike capability. This should give added deterrence to any would be adversary.

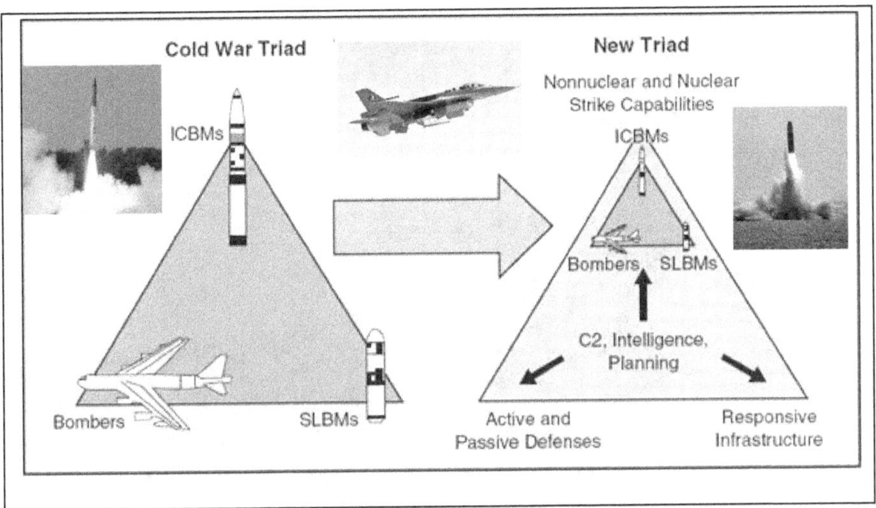

Nuclear weapons can be delivered by a number of ways to ensure survivability and also giving a nation a second strike capability.

Pakistan's 'Nasr' Land based battlefield nuclear capable missile

France's Rafael Multi-role combat aircraft, with the ability to launch nuclear weapons by air.

North Korean 'underwater test-fire of strategic submarine ballistic missile'

Nuclear arsenals

Country	Date of first test	Delivery methods
The five nuclear-weapon states under the NPT		
United States	16 July 1945	Nuclear triad
Russia	29 August 1949	Nuclear triad
United Kingdom	3 October 1952	Sea based
France	13 February 1960	Sea and air-based
China	16 October 1964	Nuclear triad
Non-NPT nuclear powers		
India	18 May 1974	Nuclear triad
Pakistan	28 May 1998	Nuclear triad
North Korea	9 October 2006	Sea and Land-based
Undeclared nuclear powers		
Israel	Not Known	Nuclear triad

The weapons possessed by the above nuclear powers are deemed to be
more destructive than the bombs dropped in August 1945 on Hiroshima
and Nagasaki in Japan. Today's weapons have become more sophisticated
and compact compared to earlier versions and their destructiveness will
ensure that millions of people could get killed in the event of a single high
yield nuclear bomb attack.

There has not been a total elimination of these nuclear weapons, as per the
NPT – all countries possessing nuclear weapons should eventually eradicate
this in a reasonable and timely manner. This is to ensure that the spread or
proliferation of nuclear weapons does not increase. The more countries that

have intentions of developing nuclear weapons to enhance their security will in a result force its adversaries to embark on similar projects and hence create further instability with more destructive levels of damage done if these nations were to go into a full-scale nuclear conflict.

Over 93% of the nuclear weapons are kept by the USA and Russia, the remaining numbers with the other nuclear powers. In addition, the North Atlantic Treaty Organisation (NATO), which is a western organisation that was initially created to counter the Warsaw pact nations of Eastern Europe and the then Soviet Union – has deployed nuclear weapons in the following five countries, Belgium, Germany, Italy, Netherlands and Turkey. This creates further risks in the use of nuclear weapons.[1]

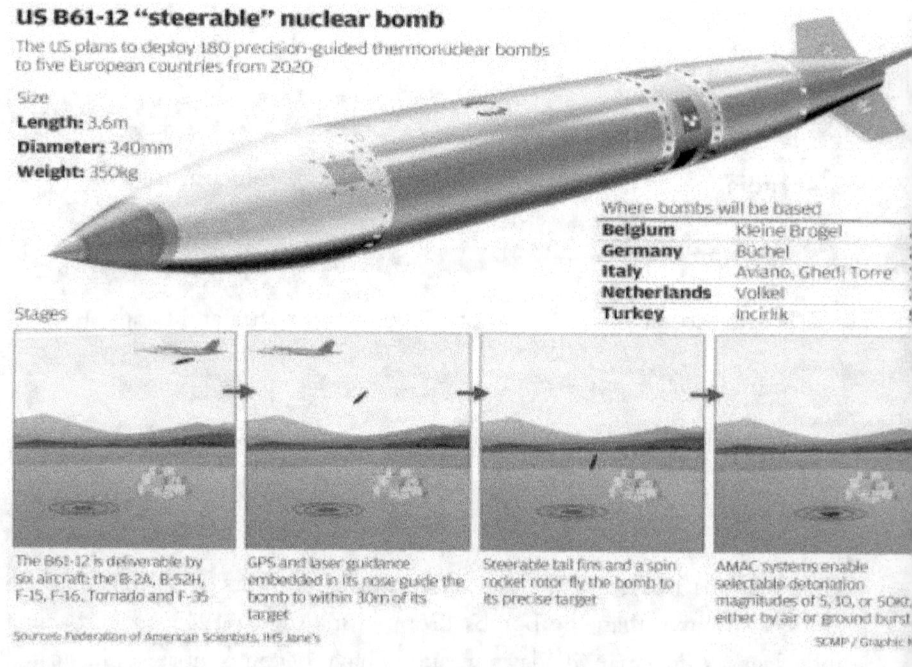

US Conducts Field Test Of New More Sophisticated Nuclear Bomb

---

[1] http://www.icanw.org/the-facts/nuclear-arsenals/

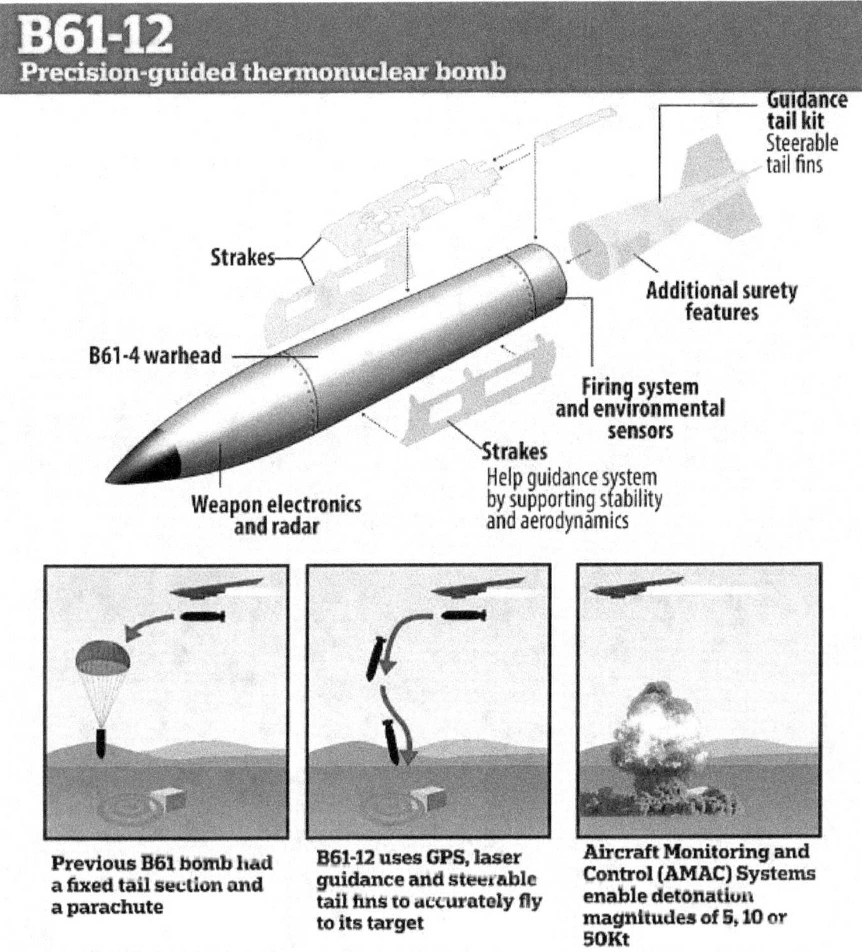

US Conducts Field Test Of New Nuclear Bomb

Though, the US and other declared nuclear powers have reduced their nuclear stockpiles, they have unfortunately continued to improve the sophistication of its new devices – smaller and more potent. They are asking others not to develop nuclear weapons but on the contrary are developing their own. This is causing much mistrust across the globe in regards to the intentions of these nuclear powers. It is these double standards that the majority of countries see the obvious hypocrisy in these major nuclear powers.

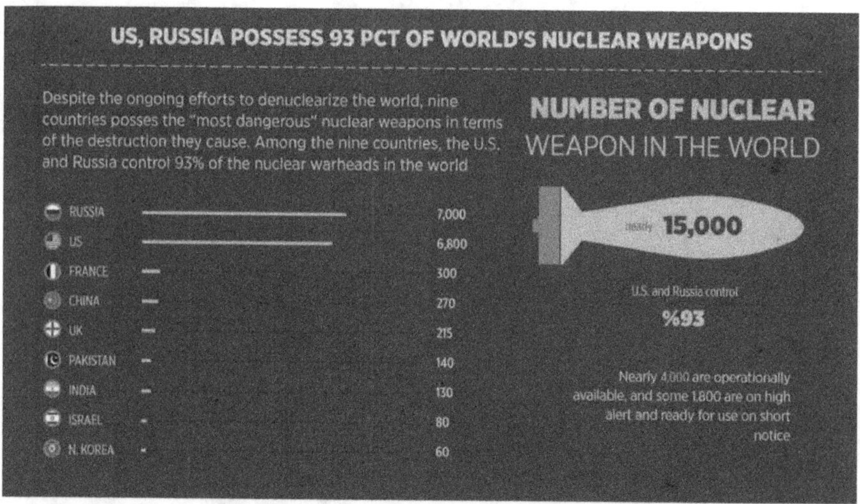

USA and Russia have 93% of the worlds nuclear weapons.

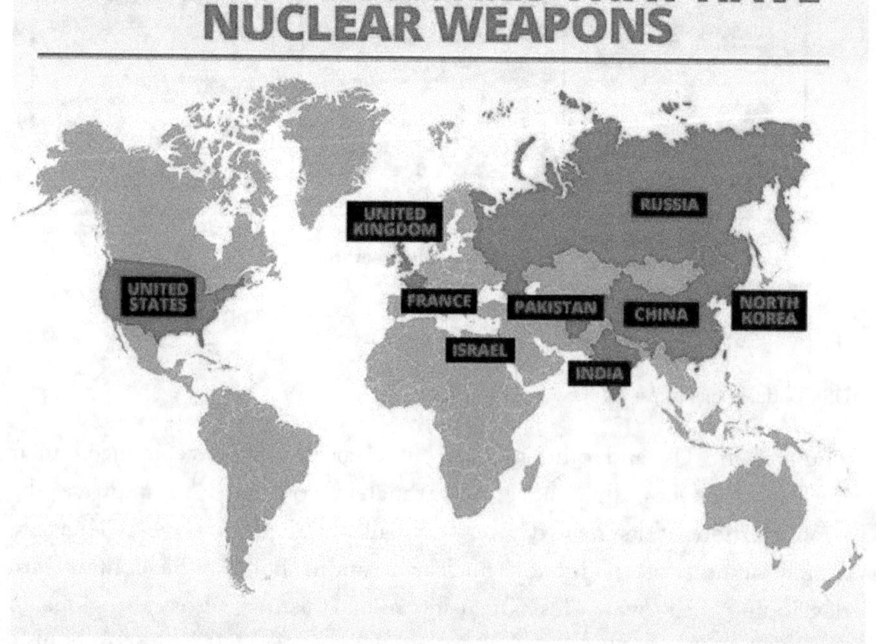

Nuclear weapons map[2]

---

[2] https://www.express.co.uk/travel/articles/889871/map-countries-nuclear-weapons-us-north-korea-

https://www.ploughshares.org/file/2801

The above chart shows the high costs in acquiring, developing and maintaining these nuclear weapons.

The next example shows that, as of 2012 the US nuclear bombs were 41,000 times more destructive than in 1945. By 2018 the weapons have become more sophisticated , smaller and with a higher yield. Enough firepower to destroy the world as we know it.

---

world-war-three

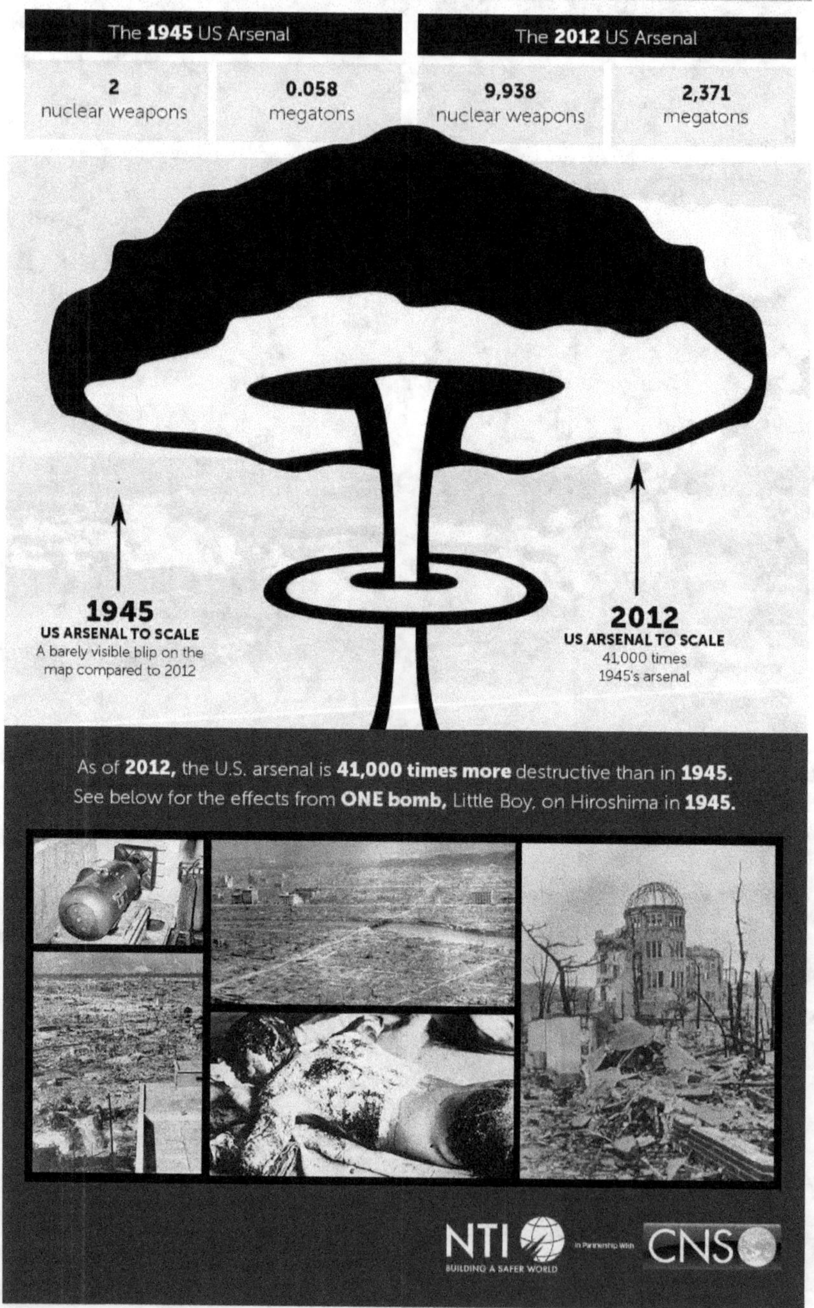

Visualizing U.S. Nuclear Firepower: 1945 vs. 2012

The 1945 US Arsenal
2
nuclear weapons
0.058
megatons

The 2012 US Arsenal
9,938
nuclear weapons
2,371
megatons

1945
US ARSENAL TO SCALE
A barely visible blip on the
map compared to 2012

2012
US ARSENAL TO SCALE
41,000 times
1945's arsenal

As of 2012, the U.S. arsenal is 41,000 times more destructive than in 1945.
See below for the effects from ONE bomb, Little Boy, on Hiroshima in 1945.

NTI
BUILDING A SAFER WORLD
In Partnership With
CNS

<u>Brief look at countries with nuclear weapons.</u>

United States of America (USA)

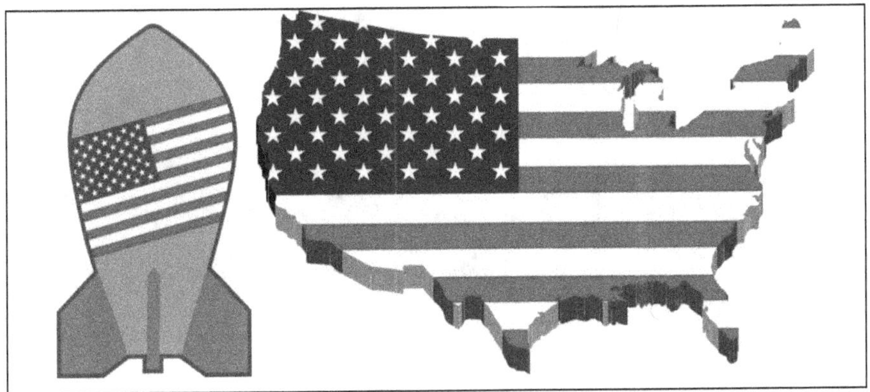

The USA was the first country to develop a nuclear bomb and currently the only country to use it against another one. It was developing nuclear weapons during World War 2 and had successfully exploded a nuclear device in July 1945. Shortly after its successful launch of the nuclear bomb, it had dropped 2 nuclear bombs on the Japanese cities of Hiroshima and Nagasaki – with a tremendous loss of life and sufferings from the after mast of a nuclear attack.

In 1967 its nuclear stockpile had reached to a massive peak of 31,225 bombs. After a number of global disarmament treaties, it had reduced its vast stockpile to a current 7,700 nuclear warheads. It has a TRIAD system in place and has the capability to attack any nation across the world and cause massive loss of life and severely damage a country's national infrastructure.

US Nuclear Triad – Second Strike Capability

US Air Force B-1 Strategic Nuclear Bombers

US Air Force Carries Out Mock Nuclear Bomb Tests in Nevada Desert

Russia

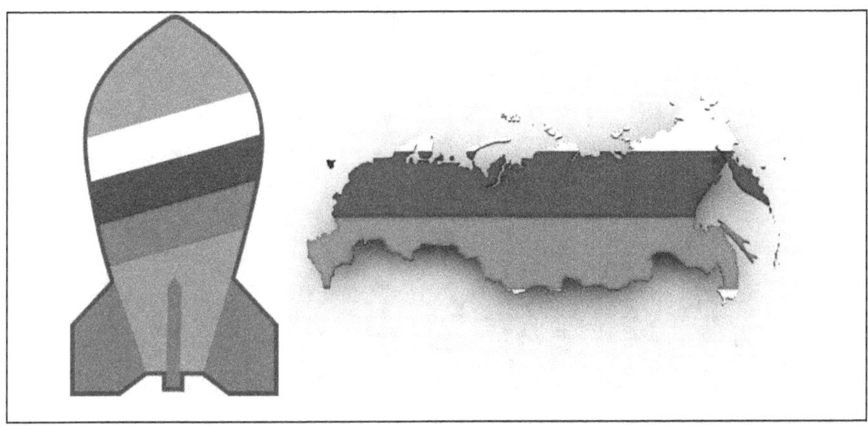

On August 1949, the former Soviet Union (USSR) had tested its first
nuclear bomb – this then had prompted the nuclear arms race with the
USA. In 1961 the USSR had detonated a nuclear device with a yield of 50
megatonnes – this was equivalent to 3,800 Hiroshima type bombs. In 1962
the USSR had conducted 79 nuclear tests during the year – its highest ever
in a year.

It is estimated that the USSR (Russian federation) had an inventory of
45,000 nuclear bombs in 1986 – but this was substantially reduced by 50%
by the late 1990s (due to the arms reduction treaty). Russia currently
possesses about 8,500 nuclear bombs and has a TRIAD capability with a
global reach.

Russia to quadruple precision strategic weapon platforms by 2021

MiG-31 jet with the Kinzhal hypersonic nuclear capable missile

Russian Tu-160 Strategic bomber increases its long-range nuclear striking power

United Kingdom

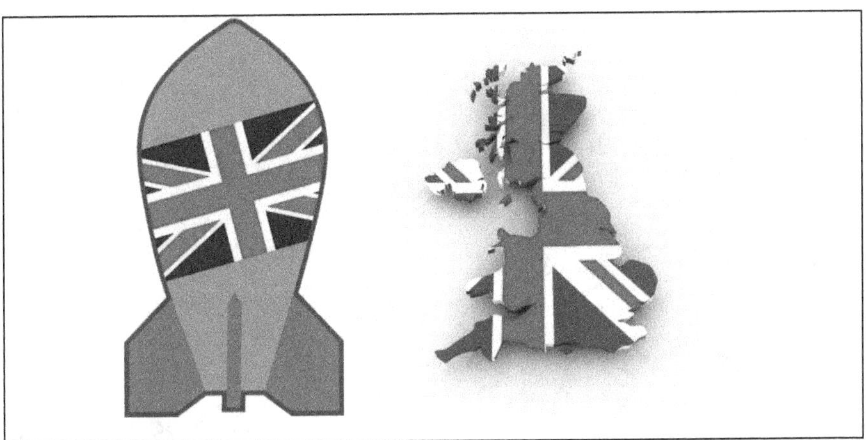

In October 1952 the United Kingdom tested its nuclear device and became
the third country to possess a nuclear bomb. The UK had conducted 45
tests but had also participated in over 1,000 nuclear tests with US nuclear
testing programme.

By 1981 the UK possessed a total of 350 nuclear bombs and by 1999 it had
reduced them to 185 warheads. Its current stockpile of nuclear bombs is
225 warheads (160 operational and 65 non-deployed warheads). The
operational warheads are primarily delivered the Trident II Submarine
Launched ballistic Missiles (SLBM) carried by the four Vanguard ballistic
missile submarines.

4 ballistic missile submarines (SSBN) carry the UK's nuclear deterrent

Britain's nuclear deterrent – Trident SLBM

UK nuclear submarine with Trident missile capability takes part in exercises in the Solent near Portsmouth

Britain's nuclear deterrent

Britain has four nuclear-powered Vanguard-class submarines, of which one is always on a three-month patrol. Each submarine carries 16 Trident missiles, each with three 475 kiloton* thermonuclear warheads

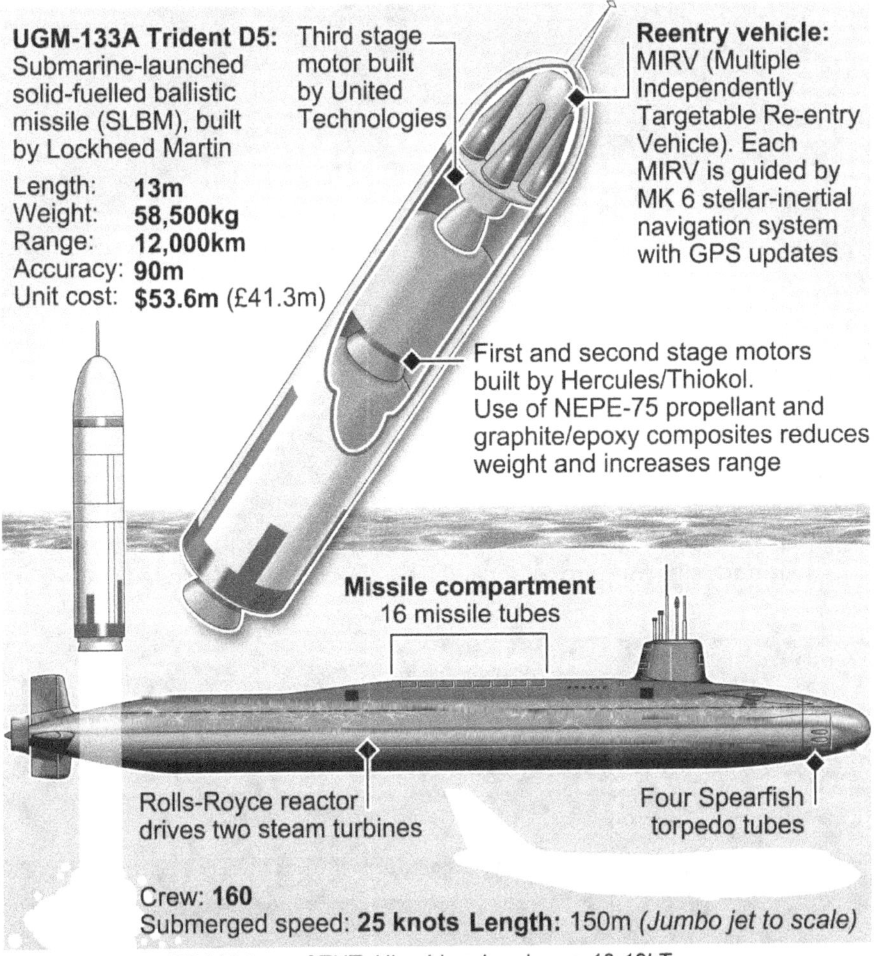

*Equivalent to 475,000 tons of TNT, Hiroshima bomb was 13-18kT
Sources: Federation of American Scientists, Sandia, 2015 Trident II DoD Budget   © GRAPHIC NEWS

Graphic shows Trident weapons system.[3]

---

[3] https://www.graphicnews.com/en/pages/34486/MILITARY-UK%E2%80%99s-Trident-nuclear-weapon

France

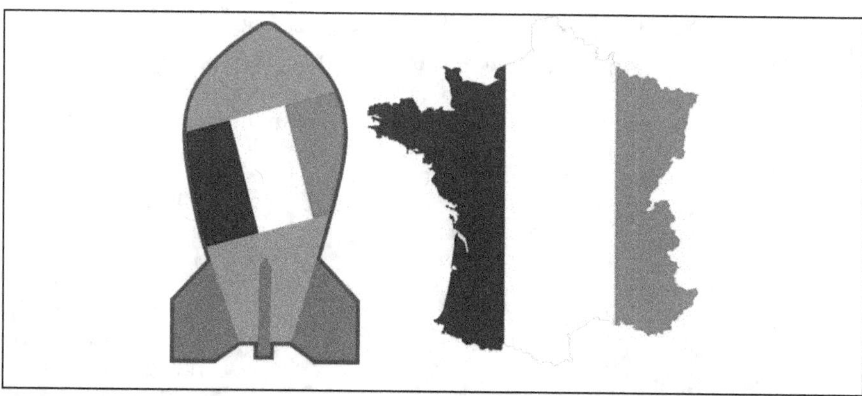

In February 1960 France became the fourth nuclear weapons country, when it successfully tested its nuclear device. France had conducted 210 nuclear tests by January 1996.

France had 540 nuclear bombs in its inventory between 1991-92. France is estimated to have deployed around 300 nuclear bombs – giving it the third biggest stockpile of nuclear bombs in the world. France uses its SLBM on its very capable Triomphant submarines and the ASMP medium range air-to-ground missiles (carried on its Rafale nuclear capable combat aircraft).

French Air Force Rafale combat aircraft with a nuclear ASMP-A missile.

Le Triomphant (S616) is the French Navy's ballistic missile nuclear-powered submarine

France Tests M51 Ballistic Missile From Nuclear-powered Submarine

China

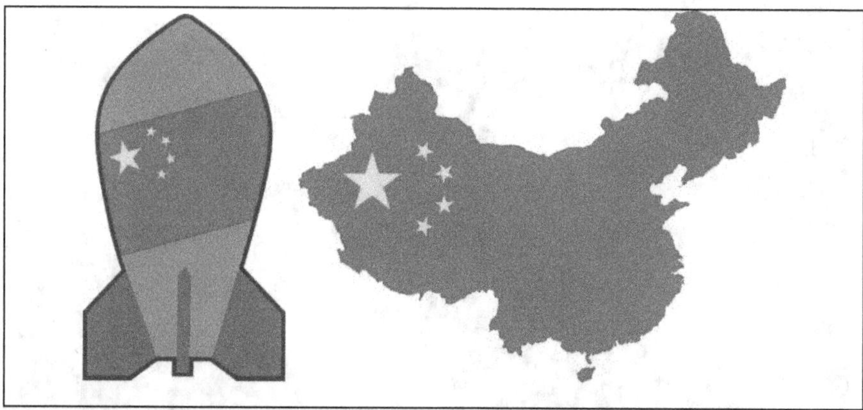

China had tested its nuclear bomb in October 1964 – making it the fifth country in the world to possess a nuclear device. China had conducted a total of 45 nuclear tests (23 atmospheric and 22 underground tests).

China had an inventory of 435 nuclear bombs in the early 1990s but had reduced the number of warheads to 240 by 2006. It has a TRIAD system of delivering its nuclear weapons by land, air and sea.

With new subs, China enters an exclusive club as one of few world powers possessing the nuclear triad

China can launch cruise missiles from its HK6 strategic bomber

China's New Stealth Bomber will complete its Nuclear Triad

India

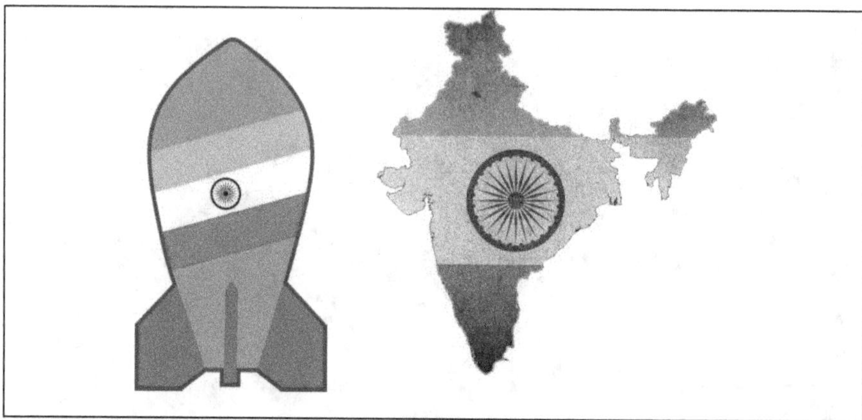

In May 1974, India had tested its nuclear bomb and thereby became the sixth nation in the world to possess a nuclear device. In addition, it conducted a number of tests in May 1998 and has an estimated 130 nuclear bombs in its inventory.

India is in the process of a completing its own TRIAD system whereby it can launch its nuclear warheads by Land, air and sea (missiles and long-range missiles).

The longer range version of India's medium-range Prithvi missile, capable of carrying nuclear

The nuclear-capable Agni-V missile is launched from Wheeler Island in Odisha.

India's first indigenous nuclear powered submarine INS Arihant which is capable of firing nuclear weapons, completing India's nuclear triad.

Indian Medium Range Agni-II Ballistic Missile

Pakistan

In May 1998, Pakistan had tested its device after India's BJP government had tested their weapon and were goading Pakistan to do the same – it became the seventh nation in the world to possess nuclear weapons.

Pakistan has an estimated 140 nuclear warheads , many are thought to be in storage. It is also developing a TRIAD system and has the ability to launch nuclear weapons through all its three services.

Pakistan's RAAD Air Launched Cruise Missile (Nuclear capable Weapon)

Pakistan's nuclear capable ballistic missile Shaheen 3

JF-17 Thunder on bombing training exercise[4]

---

[4] https://www.youtube.com/watch?v=3HhuSmSE1vI

North Korea

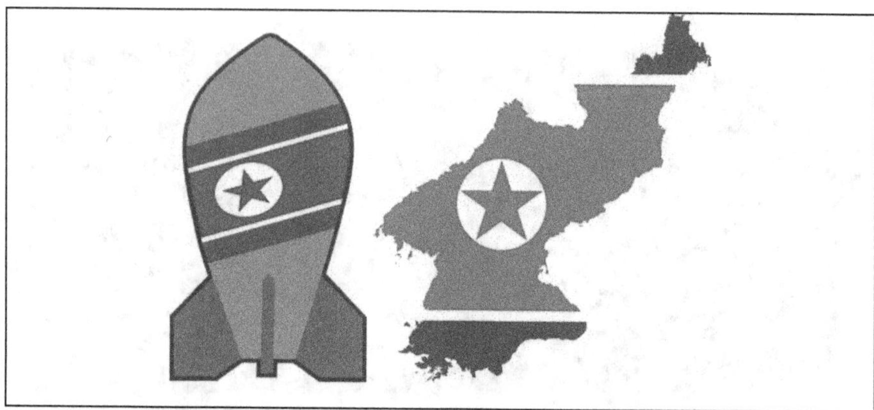

North Korea had tested its nuclear bomb in October 2006, with more tests in the future. It is thought that North Korea has an estimate of 12 – 27 nuclear warheads.

North Korea is developing a range of delivery vehicles to launch its nuclear bomb in the event of a major conflict (ballistic missiles and Submarine launched missiles).

A ballistic rocket launching drill of Hwasong artillery units of the Strategic Force of the KPA

The North Korean Musudan missile on Parade.

North Korea fired a submarine-launched ballistic missile

Israel

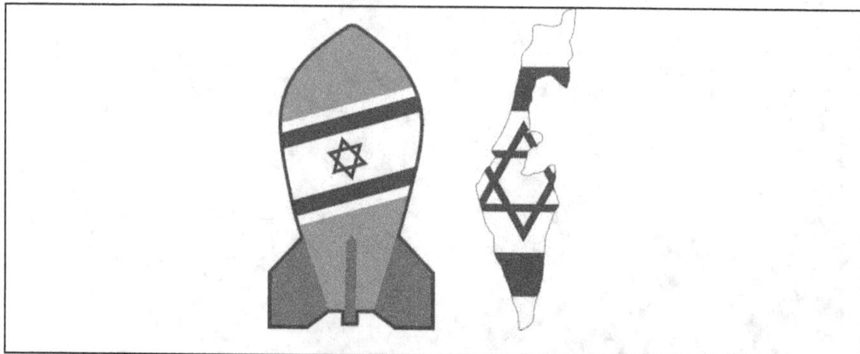

It is thought that Israel had initiated its nuclear programme in the 1950s. Israel exerts a policy of nuclear ambiguity concealing its nuclear status – it has currently not tested its nuclear bomb publicly.

Israel is estimated to have produced enough plutonium for 150-200 warheads, but is viewed to have a stockpile of 80 bombs. It has a TRIAD system to deliver its nuclear weapons by land, air and sea.

Israeli F-16 and F-15 are nuclear capable combat aircraft

The latest German-built Dolphin-class submarine INS Rahav is thought to be nuclear capable

Israeli Jericho 3 Nuclear capable missile (IRBM/ICBM)

http://www.army-technology.com/features/feature-countries-with-the-biggest-nuclear-weapon-stockpiles/

Firepower – US ability to strike any country across the world

US nuclear-powered carrier battle group, each of which carries nuclear-capable warplanes

3 NUCLEAR APARTHEID

Image/pixabay.com/Strategic B2 Stealth bomber

Nuclear Apartheid

"The double standard of insisting that we (US) can possess nuclear weapons and threaten first-strike attacks, while other nations cannot, is rightfully seen as old-fashioned hypocrisy and fuels proliferation."
Dr. Joseph Gerson in Truthout.com

The five declared nuclear weapon states are continuing an agreed system amongst themselves that is clearly based on apartheid and in addition have the veto power in United Nations Security council (UNSC), to maintain their monopoly of catastrophic destruction and blackmail. To ensure peace and security across the world, all nations must resist this monopoly and concentration of powers of apocalypse that can destroy millions across the globe (Davis, 2009).

The Indian diplomat V.M. Trivedi observed that the 'nuclear weapons club' mirrors the world's political and racial divisions. He dubbed the system 'nuclear weapons apartheid' (Farmelo, 2012). This was in reference to a small group of nuclear powers who assumed that they had the rights to have these horrific weapons but other are not allowed to enter this 'special members' club (Perkovich, 2010).

Russia's Nuclear Triad Capacity Grows With 60% of Advanced Weapons

The states that have developed nuclear arms can be divided into two categories. In the first group are the **nuclear weapon states (NWS)**, which, as defined under the Nuclear Non-Proliferation Treaty (NPT), are allowed to possess nuclear weapons – United States, Russia, China, France and the United Kingdom. In the second group are the **nuclear-armed states (NAS)** - India, Israel, North Korea, Pakistan, and South Africa, which have developed nuclear weapons outside the framework of the treaty (McDonnell, 2013).

The nuclear weapons states have had a considerable say on who is allowed to have nuclear weapons and who are not. They have consistently used bullying and arms-twisting tactics and have shown hypocrisy and double standards in order to maintain their nuclear hegemony. They have also given selected and preferential status to countries they view favourable, as in the recent case of India and this has led to a new coined term of 'neo-nuclear apartheid' by the Nuclear Command Authority (NCA) in Pakistan. The deal allows better terms and rights for India to pursue nuclear technology but with the ability to increase its stockpile of nuclear materials and hence its increase in nuclear weapons. This will destabilise Pakistan's security and hence result in Pakistan taking appropriate measures to enhance its own nuclear security (Kazmi, 2010).

The Nuclear weapons states (NWS) have succeeded in limiting the nations
with nuke making capability to a few since NPT came into force in 1968 by
allowing direct attacks , sabotage and sanctions. While the treaty required
that nations without nuclear weapons commit not to acquire them; those
with them committed themselves to move toward their elimination.
Everyone's right to develop peaceful nuclear energy was allowed. India,
Pakistan, Israel and Cuba did not sign the NPT .North Korea has been in
and then out (UNODA, 1999).

Russian Triad capability

However, the five NWS have done little towards eliminating their nuclear
arsenals. Instead they have improved upon the lethality of their nukes and
delivery systems. The West and Israel have used wars in the Middle East
and Europe to test their newer and even prohibited weapons .They have
regularly threatened and blackmailed non-nuclear nations and when it
suited, aided or acquiesced in its spread to their allies. While US led West
goes wild condemning North Korea, Iran and others, but it says little about
Israel (Singh, 2010).

Some countries in the developing world such as Iran highlight the apparent
discriminations exercised by the major nuclear weapon states. Tarock
(2006:655) argues that countries like India, Pakistan and Israel, all nuclear

weapon states and non-members of the NPT and beneficiaries of US nuclear assistance and technology, are not on the radar screen of the IAEA or of the countries (US, Britain, France, Germany) that oppose Iran's nuclear program.

Iran   USA

Iran	USA
Has never had nuclear weapons	**Has 7,200 nukes**
Is not violating the nonproliferation treaty	**Violates the NPT by not disarming, by building more, and by sharing with other nations**
Spends $24b total, $303/capita on military	Spends $648b total, $2,057/capita on military
Has 0 foreign bases and has started 0 wars in centuries	**Has >800 foreign bases in >70 countries and has invaded >70 countries in past 70 years**
Has never overthrown U.S. government	**Overthrew Iranian democracy in 1953 to install dictator**

"Iran: the seventh country on the alleged US list for regime change"

Mentioning the US's assistance to India, Tarock poses some interesting questions: "Why is it taken for granted that a nuclear Iran will be more dangerous or will act less responsibly than [countries with nuclear weapons]…And why should it be demanded only of Iran to dismantle its nuclear facilities when other countries receive assistance in the development of their nuclear capability?" (Tarock, 2006: 655).

Zbigniew Brzezinski, former national security advisor to President Jimmy Carter, stated: "The recent US decision to assist India's nuclear programme, driven largely by the desire for India's support for the war in Iraq as a hedge against China has made the US look like a *selective* promoter of nuclear weapons proliferation. This double standard will complicate the quest for a constructive resolution of the Iranian nuclear program" (Brzezinski in Tarock, 2006: 655).

In the run up to the 2005 NPT conference, a number of countries (Brazil, Egypt, Ireland, Mexico, New Zealand, South Africa and Sweden) voted for a new agenda resolution calling for implementing NPT commitments already made. However, the USA, UK and France had voted against this resolution. These preparatory talks failed even to achieve an agenda because of the deep divisions between nuclear powers that refuse to meet their own disarmament commitments (Carter, 2005).

US president Jimmy Carter

The former US president Jimmy Carter admitted that the USA is the major culprit in this erosion of the NPT. He stated that American leaders have not only abandoned existing treaty restraints but have plans to develop new weapons and have threatened first use of nuclear weapons against non-nuclear states (Carter, 2005).

Desmond Tutu

Desmond Tutu the Nobel peace laureate stated that the world must not tolerate a system of nuclear apartheid in which it is considered legitimate for some states to possess nuclear arms but patently unacceptable for others to seek to acquire them. He argued that such a double standard is no basis for peace and security in the world. The Nuclear Non-Proliferation Treaty is not a license for the five original nuclear powers to cling to these weapons indefinitely. The International Court of Justice has affirmed that they are legally obliged to negotiate in good faith for the complete elimination of their nuclear forces (Tutu, 2011).

According to Professor Jo-Ansie van Wyk, almost a third of all states that have ratified the NPT are African. All African states are state parties to the NPT (except for South Sudan) (Jo-Ansie van Wyk.2014). African states have called for the total elimination of nuclear weapons and have supported the Comprehensive Nuclear Test Ban Treaty (CTBT). Egypt in 2012 (Conference on the Weapons of Mass Destruction Free Zone in the Middle East) had expressed its disappointment in what was called the 'unilateral' postponement by organisers such as the USA (Jo-Ansie van Wyk, 2014).

Jo-Ansie van Wyk states that the African states strongly support the NPT but maintain that the NPT discriminates between NWS and NNWS states regarding their nuclear capability and access to the peaceful uses of nuclear energy (Jo-Ansie van Wyk, 2014). It is therefore imperative that the abolition of nuclear weapons is promptly pursued. Nuclear disarmament needs to be robustly implemented, with the aim of dismantling all nuclear weapons – South Africa is the ideal role model in this area.

South Africa is the only country so far that has relinquished its nuclear weapons and programme and destroyed its own nuclear bombs (estimated to have between 6-7 bombs) and has strongly advocated and adhered to the global NPT treaty and eventually the desire to have a Nuclear weapons free zone for the whole African continent. This is a model that could be applied to other continents (Goodson, 2012). Professor Jo-Ansie van Wyk argues that South Africa has not reversed its decision on the dismantlement of its nuclear weapons due to its conduct on nuclear diplomacy using niche diplomacy as a diplomatic practice (Jo-Ansie van Wyk., 2015).

Hence, South Africa has shown a working model for nuclear disarmament that could be replicated across other regions. The NWS need to take action and lead from the front – this is the only viable way for complete global disarmament.

Bomb casings at South Africa's abandoned Circle nuclear bomb production facility near Pretoria.

The five declared nuclear powers are trying to keep many potential countries from acquiring this technology, especially to the countries it considers its foes. For example, the USA sees North Korea and Iran as a major threats to its security. It has put tremendous pressures on these countries to not pursue a nuclear programme, this is despite the fact that the countries that it favours have had the US turn a blind eye, such as the Israeli acquisition of nuclear weapons (Charles Koch Foundation, 2017).[5]

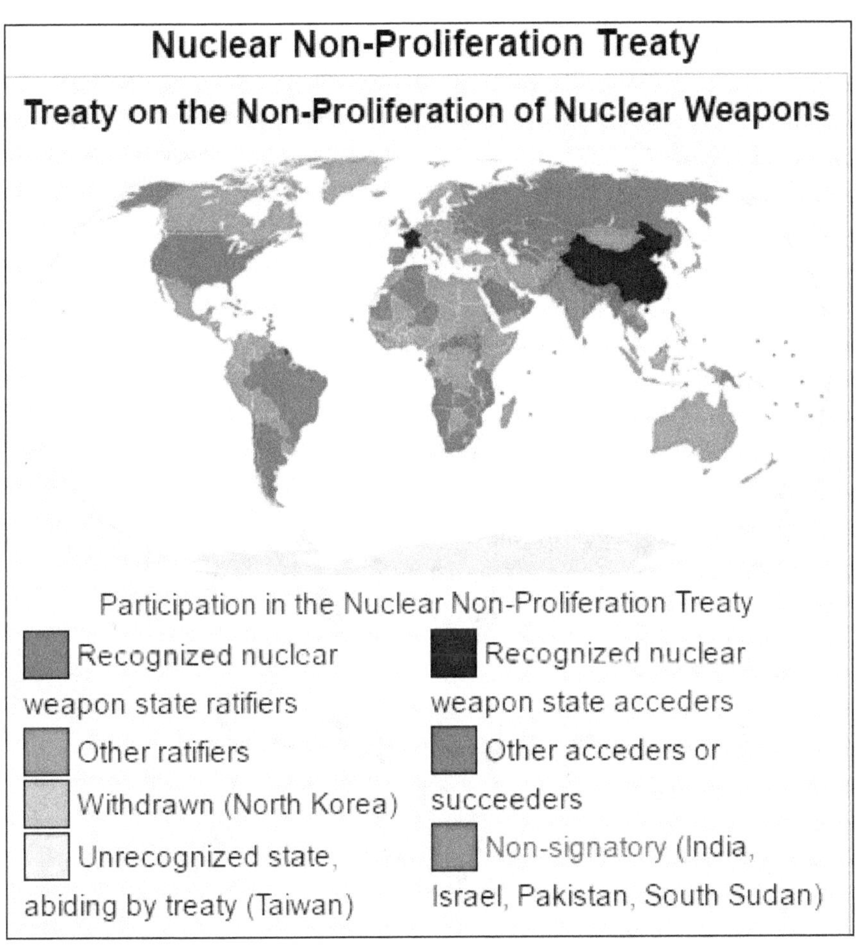

---

[5] Why the World May Be Safe with More Nuclear Weapons, Not Fewer - https://bigthink.com/charles-koch-foundation/a-safer-world-is-one-where-americas-enemies-hold-onto-their-nuclear-weapons

When it suits these declared powers, they tend to turn a blind eye to the nuclear programmes of its allies or countries that serve its interest. For instance India was more aligned towards the then Soviet Union but now that the geopolitics of the region has changed, the US has embraced India into its camp and has made strategic nuclear concessions that has put India into the Nuclear Suppliers Group – this is despite the fact that India is not a signatory of the NPT treaty. This has been a significant blow to the NPT treaty as instead of curtailing this the US is seemed to be rewarding countries.

It is argued that the security of one country will affect the security of another and each will justify why it needs nuclear weapons to protect. Morally one country could not justify that it requires nuclear weapons and others are not allowed. In the case of Iran and North Korea, both countries are aware of the US conventional and nuclear military might – they have seen many countries destroyed (the US has attacked on numerous occasions non-nuclear countries). This has been the impetus for them to embark on a nuclear programme. For Iran, it sees itself surrounded by hostile American nation, who has military troops and equipment based in many countries around it.

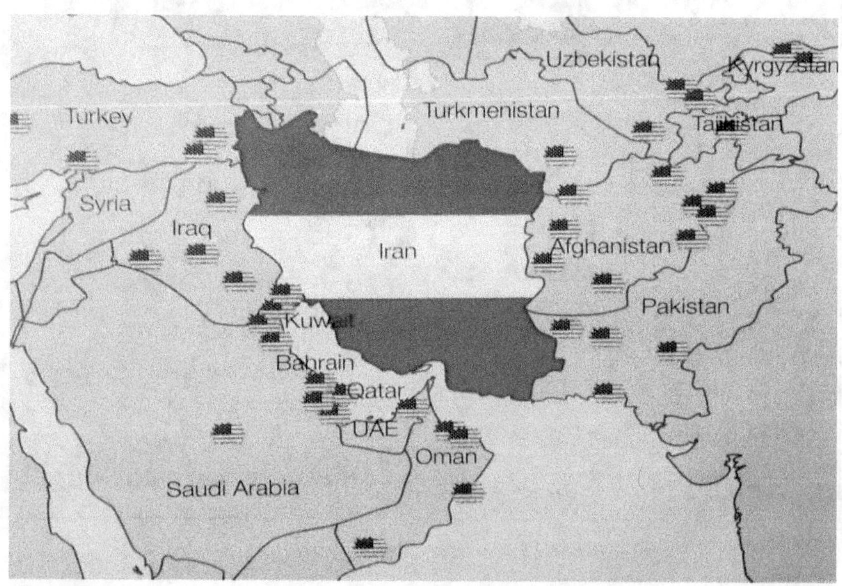

The map above depicts the US forces based around Iran.[6]

---

[6] Why the World May Be Safe with More Nuclear Weapons, Not Fewer - https://bigthink.com/charles-koch-foundation/a-safer-world-is-one-where-americas-enemies-hold-onto-their-nuclear-weapons

According to Barry Posen (Director of MIT's Security Studies Program), stated the following, **"the U.S. has its guns pointed at aspiring nuclear weapons states in a way that makes them feel even less secure".**

Many countries around the world are alert of the American military superiority in conventional as well as in nuclear capability. They have seen the regime changes undertaken to countries, such as Iraq, Libya, Syria etc. under the pretext of many things (humanitarian intervention, terrorism, Human rights etc.).

Many countries across the world are aware of America's huge nuclear arsenal—and of the fact that it's capable of annihilating any nation at a moment's notice. This fear is one of the reasons that some countries are pursuing a nuclear programme – essentially to enhance their own security (Charles Koch Foundation, 2017).

For example, North Korea's testing of its nuclear device has made the US much more hesitant in invading its borders. Unlike the states the US invaded and subsequently destroyed were all non-nuclear states. This is also what Iran sees – it probably needs the nuclear programme to deter a potential attack from a nuclear adversary and its allies, such as the USA and Israel (both nuclear powers). Charles Koch Foundation (2017) argue that, "It makes perfect sense that America's enemies would be scrambling to develop nuclear weapons—not so they can fire them, but so they can also enjoy the benefits of deterrence".

Barry Posen, is also concerned with a number of issues, "I worry about not nuclear weapons in the hands of states, but nuclear weapons that are not in the hands of states. I worry about nuclear weapons that are lost, nuclear weapons that are stolen, nuclear weapons that are poorly aligned, nuclear weapons that are sold off the back of trucks."

The above concerns are in light of incidents across the world, but primarily by the US military – it has had 32 nuclear weapons accidents which are also known as 'Broken Arrows'. There are many nuclear weapons that are still missing. Initially the US was looking at the former Soviet Union as a place of losing nukes when it had broken up into different territories – this shows that the US needs to secure its own devices before it starts looking elsewhere and pointing fingers at other nations (Charles Koch Foundation, 2017).

Mark 17 bomb, one of which was accidentally dropped by the U.S. in 1957.

Do Nuclear Weapons Provide Security?

The fear and mistrust amongst nations that possess nuclear weapons and those that do not have pose a constant threat to all people. As more and more countries seek security and are trapped in a security-insecurity paradox – where the actions of one nation contributes to the instability of the other nation. Both nations end up in a vicious cycle of escalating their defence requirements to ensure that their deterrence has not been compromised - these mistrusts ends up eating a significant amount of a country's limited natural budget.

According to ICANW, **"Nations still cling to the misguided idea of 'nuclear deterrence', when it is clear that nuclear weapons only cause national and global insecurity. There have been dozens of documented instances of the near-use of nuclear weapons as a result**

of miscalculation or accidents".[7] It further provides a table in regards to
the Myth and Reality of the security case.

MYTH	REALITY
It's OK for some countries to possess nuclear weapons.	When it comes to nuclear weapons, there are no safe hands. So long as any country has these weapons, others will want them, and the world will be in a precarious state.
It's unlikely that nuclear weapons will ever be used again.	Unless we eliminate nuclear weapons, they will almost certainly be used again, either intentionally or by accident, and the consequences will be catastrophic.
Nuclear weapons provide a useful deterrent against attack.	Nuclear weapons do not deter terrorists. Nuclear-armed nations are actually more vulnerable to pre-emptive strike and terrorist targeting than non-nuclear countries.
Nuclear weapons can be used legitimately in war.	Any use of weapons would violate international humanitarian law because they would indiscriminately kill civilians and cause long-term environmental harm.

Table: Myth and Reality of the security case[8]

Cost of Nuclear weapons and global Poverty

Researchers have predicted that over $1.739 trillion dollars are spent on
military expenditure and arms worldwide. This would also include a
significant amount spent on the development and maintenance of nuclear
weapons. This increase in a massive spending on weapons (conventional

---

[7] http://www.icanw.org/why-a-ban/arguments-for-a-ban/

[8] http://www.icanw.org/why-a-ban/arguments-for-a-ban/

and nuclear) increases the probability of conflict occurring and can therefore be a threat to peace (SIPRI Year Book 2018).

According to ICANW, "Nuclear weapons programmes divert public funds from health care, education, disaster relief and other vital services. The nine nuclear-armed nations spend in excess of US$105 billion each year maintaining and modernizing their nuclear arsenals. The US alone spends more than US$60 billion annually, and the British government's plans to replace its ageing fleet of nuclear-armed Trident submarines could cost taxpayers over £100 billion".[9]

The resulting nuclear arms competition increase political tension. In extreme circumstances, one of the nations may conclude that war is inevitable, that the balance of power is likely to worsen in the future, and that it should take pre-emptive military action to remove the threat poised against it. For example: that of Pakistan and India.

PAF F-16B dual seat combat aircraft

Pakistan had purchased some expensive fighter aircraft (F-16s) from the USA in the early 1980s and therefore had qualitatively improved its air forces offensive capabilities. In return India bought advanced fighter

---

[9] Ibid

aircraft from France (Mirage 2000s) and Russia (Mig-29s) in order to counter Pakistan. Also in other defence related areas, each side continued buying advanced and therefore very expensive systems. From tanks, ballistic missiles and eventually to nuclear weapons and despite this, still both countries were buying more firepower – the acquisition of further arms was actually undermining their security. It was really to all intents and purposes making them more insecure. The insecurity that had resulted could on the balance of probabilities lead to a potential war with terrible devastation for both countries (Cordesman, 1988).

IAF Su-30MKI multi-role combat aircraft releasing its bombs

Both of the above countries are very poor and experience many domestic problems. Poverty, child labour, homelessness are a few serious issues internally for both countries. The money they spend in arms could be utilised to improve the conditions of its people, and try and eradicate poverty and diseases, provide education and have adequate health facilities for its people.

It can be stated that the nuclear arms trade has affected governments in that it has stimulated and indirectly persuading them to spend more money on buying and developing nuclear arms, rather than spending that money to improve the quality of life of its people (Freedman, 1985).

The nuclear arms trade is such that it has become a mechanism to spend more money to defend citizens against a possible attack, rather than spending money against everyday ravages of poverty, life threatening diseases, and social issues such as employment in many countries.

The nuclear arms race amongst nations tends to divert funds from addressing current needs but it has a long term effect on issues like productivity in civilian industries, price hikes, a slowing economy etc. It can be concluded that the nuclear arms race has become a mechanism to divert vital funds from significant issues such as poverty and hunger. Hunger has a detrimental effect and many countries currently are facing huge problems. According to some sources (WHO) over **800 million individuals are chronically undernourished, and face a long and gruelling death**. Death related to hunger and starvation average 50,000 a day. In Africa alone, 5 million children died from hunger-related causes.

Key numbers

Hunger and food security
- According to WHO, the overall number of hungry people in the world: 815 million, including:
  - In Asia: 520 million
  - In Africa: 243 million
  - In Latin America and the Caribbean: 42 million
- Share of the global population who are hungry: 11%
  - Asia: 11.7%
  - Africa: 20% (in eastern Africa, 33.9%)
  - Latin America and the Caribbean: 6.6% (World Health Organization, 2017).

Malnutrition in all its forms
- Number of children under 5 years of age who suffer from stunted growth (height too low for their age): 155 million
  - Number of those living in countries affected by varying levels of conflict: 122 million
- Children under 5 affected by wasting (weight too low given their height): 52 million
- Number of adults who are obese: 641 million (13% of all adults on the planet)
- Children under 5 who are overweight: 41 million
- Number of women of reproductive age affected by anaemia: 613 million (around 33% of the total)

The impact of conflict
- Number of the 815 million hungry people on the planet who live in countries affected by conflict: 489 million
- The prevalence of hunger in countries affected by conflict is 1.4 - 4.4 percentage points higher than in other countries
- People living in countries affected by protracted crises are nearly 2.5 times more likely to be undernourished than people elsewhere (World Health Organization, 2017).

http://www.who.int/news-room/detail/15-09-2017-world-hunger-again-on-the-rise-driven-by-conflict-and-climate-change-new-un-report-says

Rich and Poor gap

Moreover, the arms trade and nuclear weapons development and storage also effects the distribution of economic growth that does occur. It contributes significantly to the widening of the gap between the rich and poor countries, a focal point of increasing world tensions and anxiety. The poorest nations suffer from the deepening military competition between them.

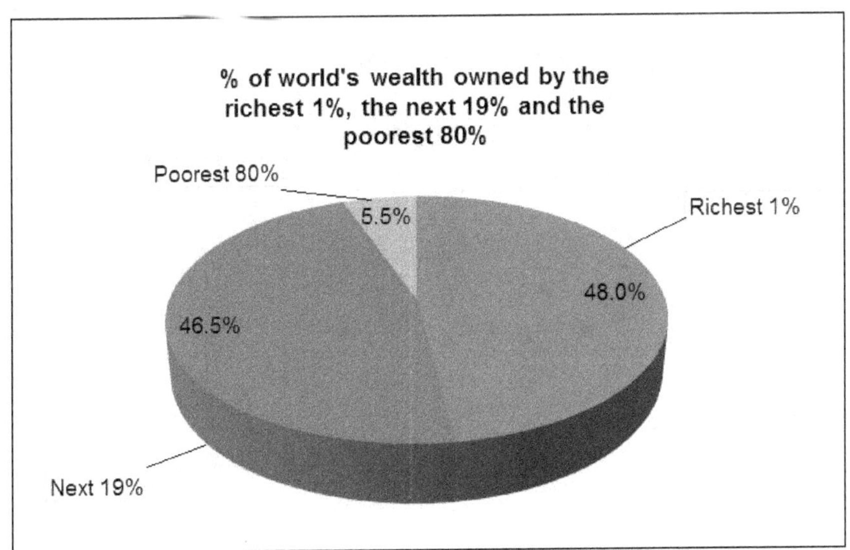

Source Oxfam

Oxfam calculated that the richest 1% of people in the world owned nearly half (48%) of the world's wealth. The vast majority of the remaining 52% of the world's wealth was owned by the next 19% of the world's richest people leaving just 5.5% of the world's wealth for the poorest 80% of people in the world.[10]

Overall, the nuclear arms race has affected the world in large, in many ways. It has caused more tensions between nations and has largely made them more insecure. It has diverted funds from necessary needs to buying weapons of destruction.

(Left) Inequality—the gap between the rich and the poor

Poverty

---

[10] (source - https://sustainingcommunity.wordpress.com/2015/01/21/even-it-up/)

Poverty – Who is responsible?

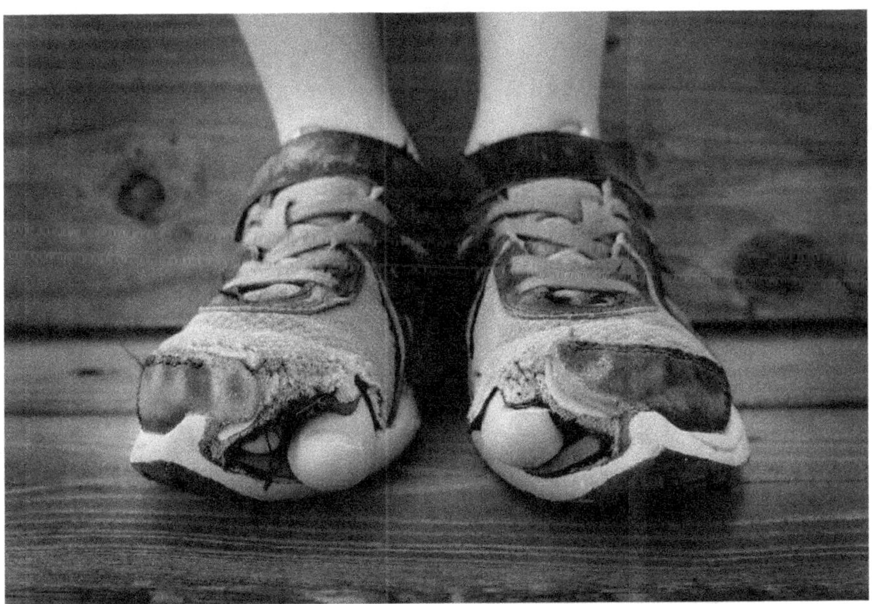

Poverty is a state of impoverishment, lack, or scarcity of certain resources that the individual
or country needs to achieve and sustain good health, happiness, and well-being.[11]

---

[11] https://gibbshappinessindex.com/articles/1087/

In addition, to the above, Nuclear weapons have caused and will cause catastrophic future environmental degradation in the event of a major conflict. No effective humanitarian response would be possible, and the effects of radiation on human beings would cause misery and death many years after the first explosion.

According to the International Committee of the Red Cross (2010), "Nuclear weapons are unique in their destructive power, in the unspeakable human suffering they cause, in the impossibility of controlling their effects in space and time, and in the threat they pose to the environment, to future generations, and indeed to the survival of humanity."

According to ICANW, "Nuclear weapons are the only devices ever created that have the capacity to destroy all complex life forms on Earth. It would take less than 0.1% of the explosive yield of the current global nuclear arsenal to bring about devastating agricultural collapse and widespread famine. The smoke and dust from fewer than 100 Hiroshima-sized nuclear explosions would cause an abrupt drop in global temperatures and rainfall".

The double standards on nuclear weapons needs to be stopped and all countries need to dismantle their nuclear weapons to ensure a more peaceful world. No country has the moral right to have these horrendous weapons that could cause catastrophic damage to the world and a massive loss of life.

To eradicate these weapons - then there can be no favoritism of which nation is allowed to develop and which one is not. There should be gradual reduction of nuclear weapons from all nuclear powers and a more robust NPT treaty where it becomes a crime for any nation which does not adhere to it – in unity lies strength against any rogue nuclear power state.

4 WMD THREATS AND PROLIFERATION

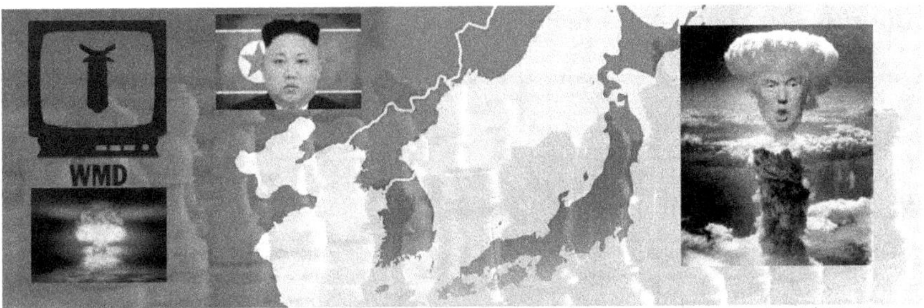

Image/pixabay.com/North and South Korea/Atomic bomb/Liberty mushroom cloud/US Trump threats/North Korean Kim Jong-Un

Since the end of the Cold War period, nuclear weapons have been reduced from a massive 70,300 warheads in 1986 to an estimated 14,550 bombs in 2017.[12] In 2017 the following nine countries possessed nuclear weapons and all have been developing a number of methods to launch nuclear weapons to deter any would be adversary (land-based intercontinental ballistic missiles, strategic bombers, and submarine-launched ballistic missiles) - the USA, Russia, UK, France, China, India, Pakistan, Israel and North Korea possess nuclear weapons.[13]

All the nuclear powers have either developed or are in the process of developing different technologies to ensure that they are able to deter a would be adversary. New ballistic missiles, air launched cruise missiles (ALCM), ground (GLCM) and sea based nuclear delivery systems are being pursued by the nuclear powers.[14]

Any war amongst the nuclear powers such as the USA and Russia would result in total annihilation. We will look into brief details of other regions, such as East Asia, South Asia and the Middle East - to highlight the mistrust of the regional players and the fear that a conflict could result in a nuclear holocaust with massive loss of life and environmental degradation. North Korea, China and Taiwan, India, Israel and Pakistan and its impact will be looked at in detail.

---

[12] https://fas.org/issues/nuclear-weapons/status-world-nuclear-forces/

[13] https://www.sipri.org/media/press-release/2017/global-nuclear-weapons-modernization-remains-priority

[14] https://www.armscontrol.org/factsheets/Nuclearweaponswhohaswhat

Table 1. World nuclear forces, 2017

Country	Year of first nuclear test	Deployed warheads*	Other warheads	Total 2017
USA	1945	1,800	5,000	6,800
Russia	1949	1,950	5,050	7,000
UK	1952	120	95	215
France	1960	280	20	300
China	1964		270	270
India	1974		120–130	120–130
Pakistan	1998		130–140	130–140
Israel	. .		80	80
North Korea	2006		10-20	10-20
Total		4,150	10,785	14,935

* Deployed warheads refers to warheads placed on missiles or located on bases with operational forces. ** Other warheads refers to warheads that are held in reserve or that are retired and awaiting dismantlement. SIPRI Yearbook 2017.

Global nuclear weapons modernisation remains priority

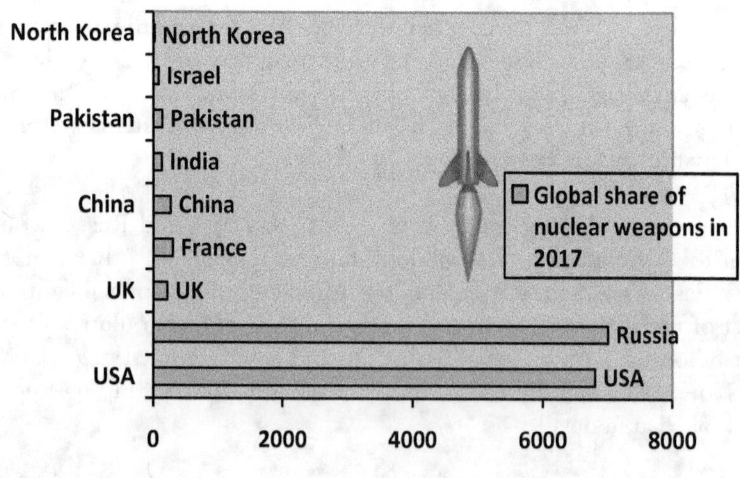

15

---

15 https://www.sipri.org/media/press-release/2017/global-nuclear-weapons-modernization-remains-priority

USA	Russia	UK	France	China	India	Pakistan	North Korea	Israel
6,800	7,000	215	300	270	130	140	20	80

https://fas.org/issues/nuclear-weapons/status-world-nuclear-forces/

Weapons of Mass Destruction

The proliferation of weapons of mass destruction (nuclear, biological, and chemical) and the missiles to deliver them pose a significant threat to the countries of East Asia. For instance there is evidence to support that North Korea has the ability to assemble a nuclear device in addition to developing long range nuclear capable ballistic missiles, such as the Nodong and the Taepo Dong 2 which have ranges from 1000km-4000km. Fired from North Korea these missiles could reach a significant part of East Asia including Japan.[16] It has further developed its new improved missiles – the Hwansong that has the capability to strike at US mainland (ICBM).

---

4.   Bearman, op cit:166

Images/pixabay.com/North Korean Ballistic missiles parade/Ballistic missile test/Military aircraft formation

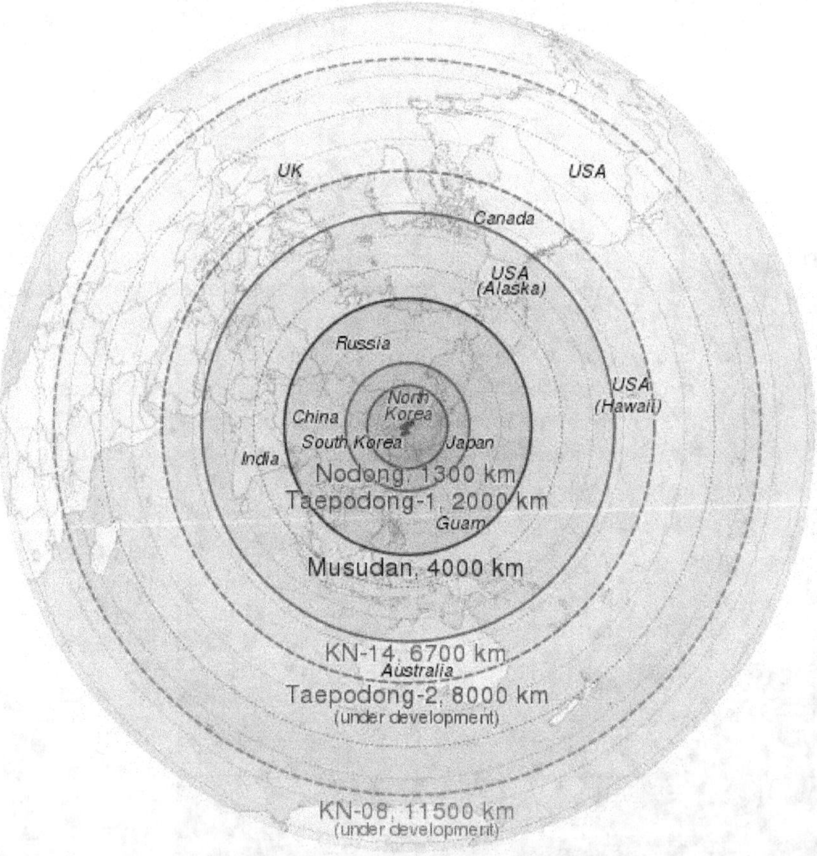

Images/commons.wikimedia.org/North Korean missile range

A Number of territorial disputes also exist in this part of the region such as the claims by China and Taiwan to the Senkaku islands occupied by Japan.[17] Furthermore Japan's neighbours are also alarmed at the Japanese plutonium reprocessing program, in spite of Japanese efforts to demonstrate its

---

5.   Brown, op cit:86

intentions to use this capability for civilian energy production, they argue that the Japanese have the capacity to develop nuclear weapons in no more than a few years at most.[18] In addition the North Korean nuclear missile threat has resulted in Japan purchasing a missile defence capability, such as the American 'Patriot' anti-ballistic missile system and there are concerns over reports that if North Korea goes nuclear then Japan will go nuclear as well (as a countermeasure to the North Korean threat). This has caused concern in China that sees Japan as a potential threat in the region.[19]

China has clearly expressed its concern that if Japan obtained a Missile Defense capability, while enhancing Japanese nuclear capabilities (such as its plutonium processing program), then China would take steps to insure the adequacy of their deterrent force, presumably by constructing more nuclear warheads and more missiles. Not only would this response further increase tensions in the region, particularly concerns about China's military strength, it would increase the capacity of the Chinese to be a supplier of WMD, their delivery systems, and their means of production. [20]

Image/pixabay.com/Patriot missile defence

---

6.   Chalmers, Greene & Zhiqiong, op cit:28
7.   Brown, op cit:234
8.   Ibid

China & Taiwan

The Chinese dispute over renegade Taiwan has resulted in China refusing to rule out using force against Taiwan, for instance early in the morning of March 8,1996, China fired three nuclear-capable missiles into two areas close to Taiwan as part of missile 'tests', these tests were taking place alongside large-scale Chinese ground and naval exercises in areas near Taiwan. The exercises have featured practicing the largest airborne assault ever conducted by China, as well as a huge amphibious exercise aimed at Taiwan. Thus China and North Korea are the only Asian countries using nuclear-capable missiles to intimidate its neighbours. [21]

North Korean Nuclear and Missile tests

The belligerent stance of North Korea and the USA (including its allies) has further increased tensions in the region. North Korea seas a threat from South Korea which has been backed up by the USA. The have seen the regular military exercise from its opponents and this has further heightened its concerns. The North Korean military apparatus is not strong enough to deter larger sophisticated military powers and hence it began to develop nuclear weapons and its delivery vehicles to reduce US regional hegemony in the area.

Its development of nuclear weapons has alarmed a lot of its neighbours and has resulted in global concern in regards to its nuclear development. North Korea has had a number of sanctions that have been authorised by the United Nations Council (UN) but this has not deterred it from pursuing its goals.[22]

North Korea has tested its sixth nuclear test and has rapidly increased its missile program. In 2017 it had launched 23 missiles during its 16 tests and this has enabled it improve on the technology to ensure reliability and improved capability. It has improved its range and has controversially fired its missiles in Japan's exclusive economic zone. It is improving its short range, medium range missiles and working on an intercontinental ballistic

---

[21] The Economist, **Asian Security**, Published by the Economist Newspaper Ltd, 1996, p83

[22] http://edition.cnn.com/2017/05/29/asia/north-korea-missile-tests/index.html

missile (ICBM) missile with reach to target mainland USA.[23]

North Korea intends to deter the USA from attacking its country and undertake a regime change by sending a clear message of its ballistic missile reach of mainland USA. It believes that the USA will not try to topple the North Korean regime of Kim Jung On from power if it new that North Korea is capable of a nuclear attack on the USA mainland. Pyongyang believes Washington would not launch an attack in case of a reprisal and see its nuclear weapons as a deterrence to USA aggression. North Korea is familiar with fall of regimes in Iraq, Libya and elsewhere done by the USA.[24]

The USA see this as a threat and is trying different ways of addressing this issue. The US president, Donald Trump has threatened to "totally destroy" North Korea if his country is forced to defend itself or its allies.[25] North Korean leader Kim Jong-un has described the US president as "mentally deranged".[26]

There are approximately 28,500 US military personnel based in South Korea, divided by the 4km-wide demilitarised zone that stretches more than 250km along the border. The frequent tests of ballistic missiles by the North Korean regime and South Korean military exercises near the border with US forces has increased tensions. The North Korean regime's main goal is survival - and direct conflict with the US would seriously endanger it. A US attack on North Korea would force the North Korean regime to retaliate against US allies South Korea and Japan. This would result in a massive loss of life. In addition, it could also prompt North Korea to fire its nuclear capable ICBM missiles at the US mainland. The rhetoric coming from the North Korean and US leadership could lead to miscalculation from both sides – resulting in a catastrophic conflict in the region.[27]

---

[23] Joshua Berlinger, CNN December 4, 2017
http://edition.cnn.com/2017/05/29/asia/north-korea-missile-tests/index.html
[24] Joshua Berlinger, CNN December 4, 2017
http://edition.cnn.com/2017/05/29/asia/north-korea-missile-tests/index.html

[25] http://www.bbc.co.uk/news/world-asia-40882877
[26] http://www.bbc.co.uk/news/world-asia-40882877
[27]http://www.aljazeera.com/news/2017/05/north-korea-testing-nuclear-weapons-170504072226461.html

Therefore, it is vital that confidence building measures are introduced into the region and that tensions are gradually reduced. The region needs to amicably resolve its conflict otherwise, any misinterpreted move in the current tense environment could lead to an accidental war with horrendous results.[28]

Indo-Israel Military Nexus and Pakistan

Indian Prime minister Modi and Israeli Prime minister Netanyahu.

Another area for potential conflict is in South Asia – Pakistan's security concern is the improving military ties between India and Israel. Since formal ties were established in 1992, Israeli military exports to India have grown to over $150 million a year. From the period 2012-2016 Israeli firms sold up to $1 billion a year in sales to India on average. In fiscal 2016-18, Israel is trying to sell the sophisticated Spike anti-tank missiles - if India goes through with this deal, Israel will be for the first time the largest arms supplier to India.[29] The defence co-operation includes sophisticated pilot-

---

[28] http://www.bbc.co.uk/news/world-asia-40882877

[29] Israel likely to become India's largest arms supplier - https://www.hindustantimes.com/world-news/israel-likely-to-become-india-s-largest-arms-supplier/story-tZQFenVzYWzaQFnPqbznqM.html

less drones, night vision equipment and extending to the nuclear, ballistic missile targeting systems and spy satellite technology.[30]

India-Israel ties increased military ties and the sales of sophisticated items to the Indian armed forces has caused a lot of concern to Pakistan. Force multiplier Israeli technologies have been sold to India and agreements in development projects of military related equipment has also increased. Pakistan is especially worried about the sale of the state-of-the-art Arrow anti-missile system that gives India the potential to neutralize part of Pakistan's nuclear ballistic missile capability. In addition, the Phalcon Airborne Early Warning, Command and Control (AEW&C) system will give India the deep edge and capability to look deep into Pakistan's territory (it gives India the ability to easily detect the movement of Pakistan's combat aircraft). Also the co-development of the Barak Anti-missile system will gives the Indian Navy huge advantage in its defensive and offensive capability.[31]

The IL-76 Phalcon AWACS platform plays significant role in Indian Air Force's Network-Centric Operations

Israel has viewed that Pakistani nuclear programme with a growing sense of alarm since the 1970s. It fears an 'Islamic Bomb' either being deployed to counter Israel's nuclear and conventional security over its Arab foes, or

---

[30] Yoel Cohen, India bomb test may affect Israel Relations, Jewish Chronicle, Publishers Jewish Chronical Newspaper Ltd, May 29, 1998, Pg3

[31] India-Israel Strengthened Nexus -
http://hilal.gov.pk/index.php/layouts/item/2805-india-israel-strengthened-nexus

being transferred to an Arab country.[32] In 1981, Prime Minister Sharon of Israel indicated that the security of the Israeli entity included Pakistan.[33]

According to the journalists Adrian Levy and Catherine Scott-Clark (in their book titled *'Deception: Pakistan, the US and the Global Weapons Conspiracy'* claimed that in 1983-84 India and Israel secretly planned to attack Pakistan's nuclear facility in Kahuta (near Islamabad).[34] Israel had attempted to destroy the Kahuta plant as it had successfully destroyed the Iraqi nuclear plant in Osirak. It needed Indian help in undertaking this mission. There were strong ties between the Israeli Mossad and Indian RAW intelligence agencies. Both countries had felt that it was in their interest to undergo a preventive strike on Pakistani nuclear facility in Kahuta. A number of plans were initiated in 1982 to 1984 by Israel and India in regards to implementing this attack – however due to a number of reasons

Israeli US made F-16 combat aircraft attacking Iraqi Osiraq nuclear plant

Pakistani intelligence (ISI) had intercepted the communication of the Indo-Israeli joint plan of attacking Pakistan's Kahuta facility and took appropriate security measures. Pakistan had sent strong messages to Tel Aviv and New

---

[32] Ibid

[33] Y. Ammar, The Kashmir Factor, Palestine Times, 9 October, 1991, Pg2

[34] India, Israel almost attacked Kahuta: report -

https://www.pakistantoday.com.pk/2015/10/26/india-israel-almost-attacked-kahuta-report/

Delhi that if Kahuta is attacked by anyone they would lay nuclear waste on
Tel Aviv and New Delhi.

Pakistan's defences were put on a full alert and the Pakistani air force was
put on high alert for any incursions. It is said that the PAF Chief of air staff
had asked the Pakistani F-16 squadron if any pilot was willing to volunteer
to fly a one way mission to Tel Aviv (Pakistan couldn't have flown a sorty
to Israel as it lacked air-air-refeuling at the time), the whole PAF F-16
squadron raised their hands to volunteer.

Air Marshal M. Anwar Shamim (PAF Air Chief during that time), narrated
"that while talk of the India-Israel nexus was still in the air, he requested
Foreign Minister Sahibzada Yaqub Ali Khan to declare at an appropriate
time Pakistan's intention of retaliating if any action was taken against the
country's nuclear assets".

IAF Jaguars in conjunction with Israeli F-16s were to be the key aircraft to attack Pakistan's nuclear
facility in Kahuta.

In addition, in 1983 Dr Raja Ramanna, the then director of the Bhabha
Atomic Research Centre, was warned by the then Chairman of Pakistan
Atomic Energy Commission Munir Ahmed Khan in Vienna in the autumn
of 1983 that Islamabad would attack Trombay (Indian nuclear plant) if its
facilities in Kahuta were hit.

Furthermore, it is claimed that US intelligence satellites had detected two
Jaguar squadrons missing from Indian Ambala airbase in Indian Punjab and
moved to another location close to the Kahuta facility near Islamabad. The

information was also provided to Pakistan, reducing the element of surprise from a joint Indo-Israeli attack.

To Pakistani officials, the signs were clear – their nuclear facilities were under the threat of a preventive strike. Both the Karachi Nuclear Power Plant (KANUPP) and Kahuta were vulnerable, so President Zia tasked Chief of General Staff Mirza Aslam Beg to improve their defences. PAF planes scrambled and began combat air patrol (CAP missions), which soon became a part of the normal operational routine. Since then, the skies above Kahuta have been no- fly zones.

Pakistani Kahuta plant

In the 1980s, there were reports in both the British and Indian media of Israel requesting Indian co-operation to bomb the Kahuta reactor in Pakistan. This would have involved the use of the Indian air base at Jamnagar near the Pakistan border as a possible refuelling stop. India reportedly declined the request due to the fear of a Pakistani retaliation on its own nuclear sites.[35] Moreover in 1991, Pakistan's Interior Ministry warned Parliament of another possible joint Israeli-Indian sabotage attempt at Kahuta, which is only 20km from the Srinagar capital of Indian-held Kashmir.[36]

---

[35] Cohen, op cit:3

[36] Ammar, op cit:4

Israeli US F-16 combat aircraft

IAF Jaguar attack aircraft

According to the Indian weekly *'News Behind News'*, Major General Ivry, the second-in-command of the Israeli Defence Ministry, attempted another Israeli-Indian collaboration in 1995. He requested the use of Indian airbases at Jodhpur or Bhuj, on the basis of a *'common threat perception'*, in return for an Israeli package deal to India which included airborne warning and control systems (AWACS), remotely piloted vehicles (RPV), sophisticated radar jammers and specialised weapons, including parts of its own spy satellite technology. India turned down this package, which would almost certainly have raised fears of a Pakistani retaliation on India's own reactors.[37]

Of greater concern was Israeli-Indian nuclear co-operation. Dr Abdul Kalam, the architect of India's nuclear and ballistic missile programme, visited Israel several times, over a period of months between 1996-1997. Senior Israeli scientists also made several visits to India over the same period. The close ties between Dr Kalam and his Israeli counterparts have suggested parallels with Israel's secret co-operation with South Africa in at least one nuclear test in the late 1970s.[38]

Israeli US supplied F-16 multi-role combat aircraft

According to *The Washington Times*, Pakistan feared a combined Indo-Israeli pre-emptive air-strike as it conducted its first nuclear test on 28th May 1998,

---

[37] News International, Israel offers India AWACS for Airbases as Part of 'Common Threat Perception', Jang Publishers Ltd, April 18, 1995, Pg1

[38] Christopher Walker, Israel's Helped India for 20 Years, The Times, Thursday June 4, 1998, Pg16

in the same way that Israeli combat aircraft destroyed Iraq's Osirak nuclear reactor in 1981.[39] An F-16 fighter-bomber was spotted twice in Pakistan's airspace just before the tests. The aircraft was assumed to be part of an Israeli strike-force, as India has no F-16 aircraft in its airforce. Pakistan, suspecting that Israeli jets were using Indian bases, made preparations to counter an air-strike by placing its air-force and missiles on high alert.[40] Western defence experts did not rule out the possibility of an Indo-Israeli attack on Pakistan's nuclear facilities. According to Paul Beaver, of Jane's Information Group, the Israeli F-16s had been equipped with an advanced reconnaissance system to take high-altitude pictures of targets over a 50 miles radius. The high resolution pictures were capable of reading the lettering on the side of a truck parked at Pakistani nuclear facility.[41]

Israeli F-16 multi-role combat aircraft

Overall, Israel's offers of advance weapon systems, her help with India's nuclear and ballistic missile programme and also her assistance in providing expertise to India, to crush the uprising in Kashmir, point towards an Indo-

---

[39] Martin Sieff and Yoel Cohen, Pakistan Feared Israel's Strike during Nuclear test, Jewish Chronical, June 5, 1998, Pg3

[40] Christopher Walker and Michael Evans, Pakistan Feared Israeli Raid, The Times, Wednesday June 3, 1998, Pg3

[41] Ibid

Israeli nexus directed against Pakistan.[42]

Israeli US supplied Apache attack helicopter

Israeli F-15 Eagle combat aircraft

---

[42] Ammar, op cit:2

Pakistani MBT on exercise

Had India attacked Pakistani nuclear installations in 1984, it certainly would
have started a full-scale war. Pakistan would have retaliated in kind against
an Indian nuclear installation. The region was simply fortunate as it escaped
a fourth war that could have rapidly escalated to a nuclear war.[43]

Indo-Pakistan Nuclear Scenario (War over Kashmir)

The Indo-Pakistan dispute over Kashmir has great potential for
miscalculations to occur, this could have a disastrous impact for the region.
The risks of inadvertent nuclear war becomes more likely – with serious
global ramifications. The following is a likely scenario in Kashmir that could
easily escalate to a nuclear exchange for India and Pakistan.

Kashmir Scenario – Potential for a nuclear war

Freedom demands from Indian occupation – Civil	**1**	Heavy handed tactics by the Indian security forces – cause	**2**

---

[43] India, Israel almost attacked Kahuta: report -
https://www.pakistantoday.com.pk/2015/10/26/india-israel-almost-attacked-kahuta-report/

disturbances

Kashmiri protestors in Indian occupied Kashmir

The Kashmiri uprising in Indian occupied Kashmir is gaining popularity amongst the Kashmiri people – who are seeking freedom from Indian security forces oppression. There are over 700,000 Indian troops in Indian occupied Kashmir that are trying to

more widespread riots.

Burhan Wani was the commander of a Kashmiri militant group Hizbul Mujahideen – fighting for their freedom in Indian occupied Kashmir.

Indian security forces heavy handed and oppresive tactics on Kashmiri protestors.

Indian brutality

brutally suppress the indigenous nationalist/separatist/freedom movement. Despite India's brutal tactics, the Kashmiri movement is gaining momentum.

Militants/freedom fighters in hot pursuit from Indian troops cross the border into Pakistan. 3

Indian troops and Kasmir's rebels

Border Skirmish between Pakistan and India – due to hot pursuit of the militants/freedom fighters. Clashes occur. 4

Indian border patrols

fighting against Indian occupation
of Kashmir

Kashmir's young rebels

Pakistani border patrols

Pakistan anti-tank/anti-bunker
missile

Indian soldiers

Indian and Pakistani soldiers have
clashed on numerous occassions
on the Line of Control (LOC) in
disputed Kashmir. The clashes
have resulted in many soldiers
and civilians being killed from
both sides of the border
(primarily due artillery shelling
and small arms fire).

Limited border conflict escalates to a major full blown conflict

4th major Indo-Pakistan war starts. Indian numerical supremacy takes toll on Pakistani forces.

Indian Artillery

Pakistani firepower

Pakistani Multiple Rocket Launchers

Indian MBT and Artillery

Indian Air Force Strike aircraft

7 Pakistan begins to lose significant forces and territory – India is threatening to cross Pakistan's 'Red' line. Pakistan contemplates in the use of nuclear weapons on Indian troop formations, as a warning. It fires tactical nuclear weapons on Indian military formations – via Nasr battlefield nuclear missile. Watching an Indian response, Pakistan ready to fire its main long-range nuclear capable ballistic missiles.

8 India reacts with firing Nuclear ballistic missile – nuclear conflict erupts. India aims to destroy all known nuclear/launch sites in Pakistan. First major strike – with the plan to destroy all nuclear capability of Pakistani forces.

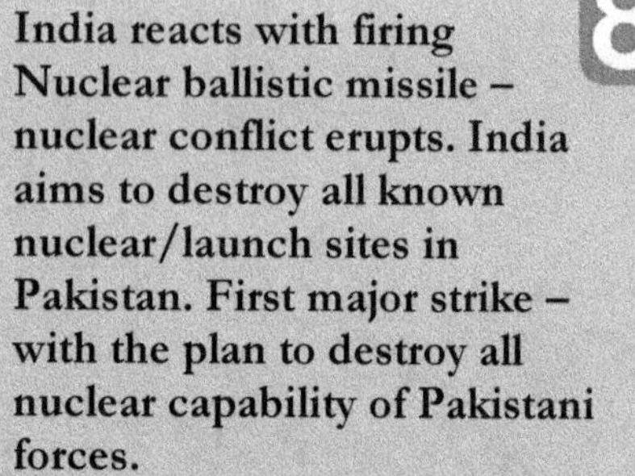

Indian Prithvi Nuclear ballistic Missile

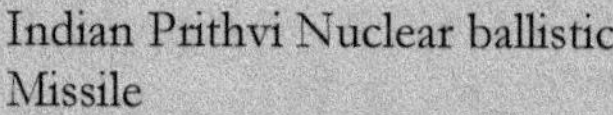

Tactical nuclear weapons

Indian Agni nuclear capable ballistic missile

Pakistan counter-attacks (second strike capability from its submarines) with SLCM or SLBM in an attempt to destroy Indian forces/cities. 9

Indian second strike capability has been initiated from its submarines – aim to destroy remaining Pakistani forces. 10

**Babur 3 SLCM (Nuclear) –
Second strike capability**

**Pakistan's RAAD Air Launched
Cruise Missile (ALCM)**

India has a second strike capability that can counter a nuclear first strike successfully.

11 Pakistani and Indian nuclear numbers are roughly 130-150 weapons each – that is approximately up to 300 nuclear weapons to use in the subcontinent. Nuclear holocaust – Armageddon for this region.

12 In the 1983 film War Games, a nuclear war simulation is accidentally started by a supercomputer designed to take over in event of the cold war spiralling out of control. After evaluating all the possibilities, the computer declares that **"war is a strange game, in which the only winning move – is not to play"**. That advice is possibly truest for Pakistan and India right now. [44]

---

[44] Raghu Raman, Why war with Pakistan—is not an option -
https://medium.com/@captraman/why-war-with-pakistan-is-not-an-option-3ccfa25a1529

11

The unthinkable nuclear nightmare!

12

Pakistan and India are now on the verge of completing their third leg of the TRIAD (air, land and sea-based nuclear weapon carrying platforms) – with Pakistan's launch of the submarine launched cruise missile (SLCM) it has validated and demonstrated its second strike nuclear capability. India has also demonstrated with its development and testing of the Submarine launched ballistic Missile (SLBM) from its nuclear submarine INS Arihant – giving it a credible nuclear second strike capability. Both countries are continuing to develop and increase the range and sophistication of its missiles.

According to Bharat Kamad (strategic analyst), "The triad becomes effective when you have a submarine operational at all times. In our case, a triad is operational only part of the time-when the Arihant sails out to sea". And further states, " When an Indian SSBN sails out of Visakhapatnam and into the Bay of Bengal, it can virtually disappear for months, remaining underwater, its endurance limited only by the endurance of its crew, communicating only through extremely low frequency (ELF) antennae which it trails in the water. While bombers, mobile missile launchers, missile trains and ground-based launchers can be tracked, nuclear submarines are virtually undetectable. This is what makes them the most precious asset of the nuclear triad".[45]

The Indian nuclear submarine, Arihant is currently being equipped with 12 B-05 SLBMs with a range of 750Km. this is further being improved by the 3,500km K-4 SLBM that is in development. In addition, India is planning for further tests of the K-5 SLBM with an estimated range of over 5,000km (the 'K' series of missiles are named after former president APJ Abdul Kalam).[46]

Pakistan continues to improve its second strike capability to deter any indian aggression – it has successfully tested the 'Babur 3' submarine launched cruise missile (SLCM) and the meduim range, Ababeel (MIRV) ballistic missile that is capable of carrying multiple warheads. The SLCM Babur missile has a range of 280 miles and is thought to be equipped with stealth technologies that will allow it to evade Indian radar and ballistic missile defense systems. The 'Ababeel' missile has a reported range of 1,367 miles and is able to carry multiple nuclear warheads with the assistance of Multiple Independent Re-entry Vehicle technology.[47]

---

[45] India Today magazine: A peek into India's top secret and costliest defence project, nuclear submarines - https://www.indiatoday.in/magazine/the-big-story/story/20171218-india-ballistic-missile-submarine-k-6-submarine-launched-drdo-1102085-2017-12-10

[46] Ibid

[47] Pakistan Improves Second Strike Capability With First Successful Submarine Ballistic Missile Launch - http://www.phcintelligencer.com/2017/03/10/pakistans-second-chance/

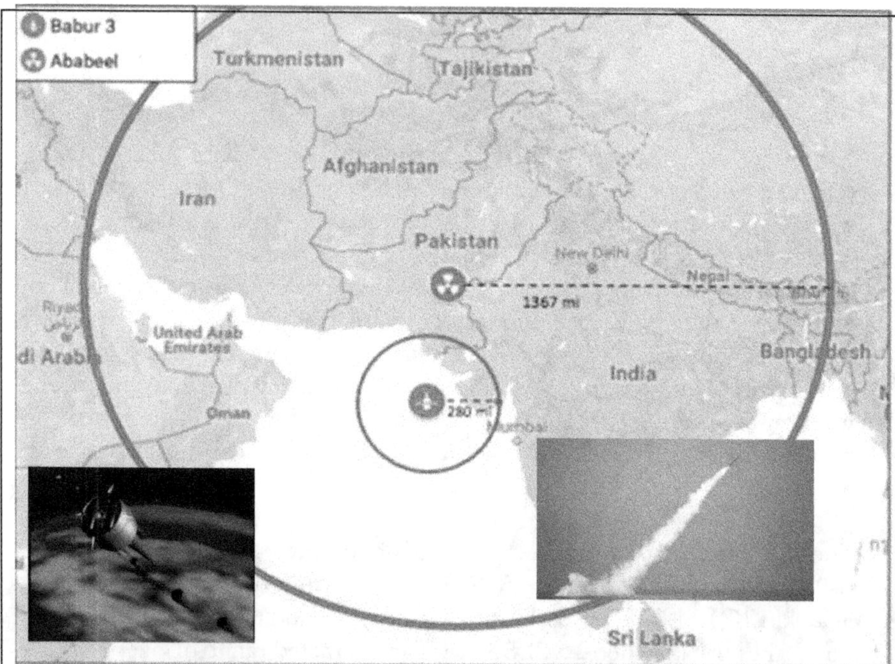

Pakistan's current range of Babur 3 SLCM and Ababeel MIRV ballistic missile – it is assessed that Pakistan will continue to extend the range and sophistication of these missiles in due course.[48]

---

[48] Pakistan Improves Second Strike Capability With First Successful Submarine Ballistic Missile Launch -
http://www.phcintelligencer.com/2017/03/10/pakistans-second-chance/

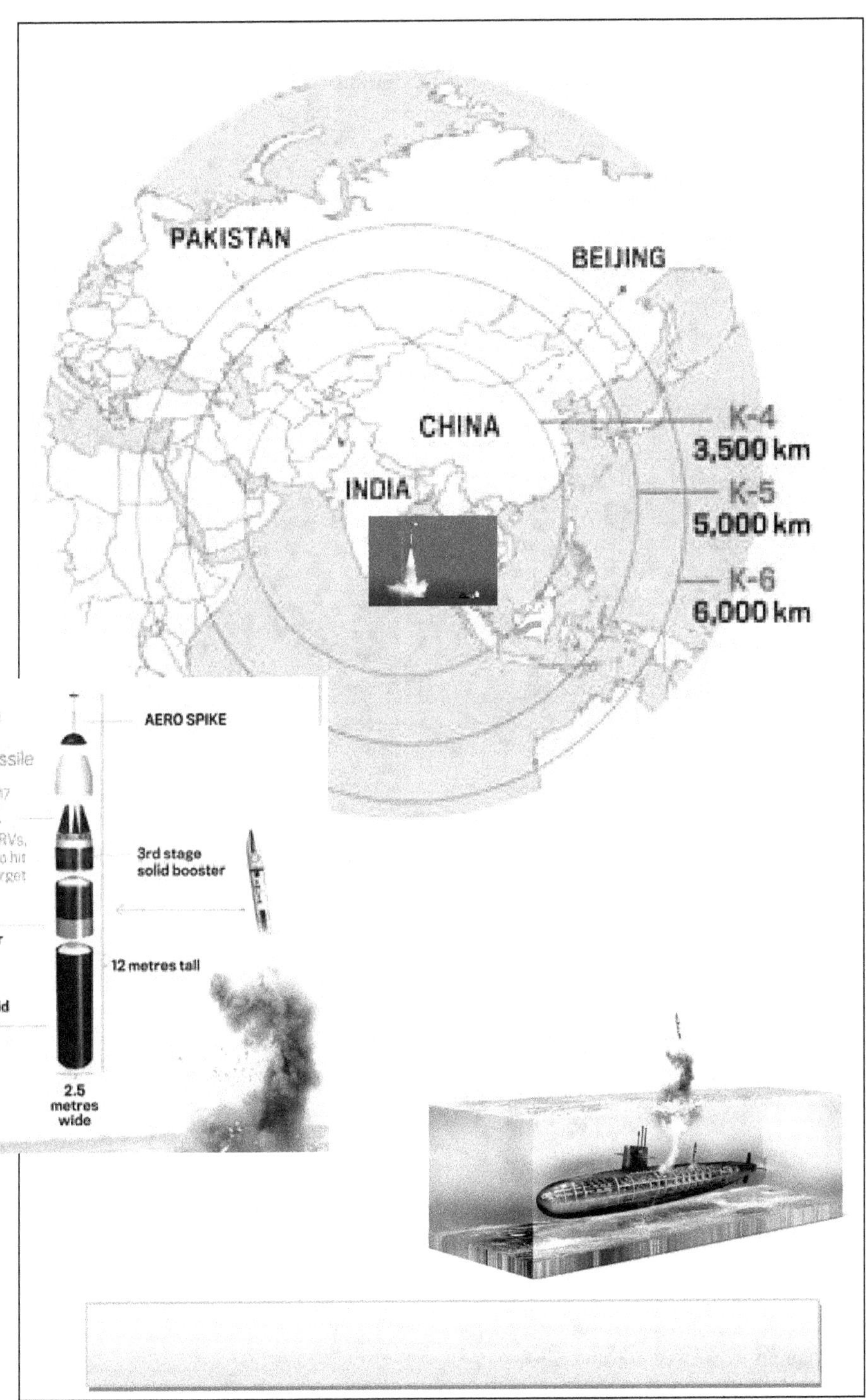
PAKISTAN
BEIJING
CHINA
INDIA
K-4
3,500 km
K-5
5,000 km
K-6
6,000 km
AERO SPIKE
rine
ed
c Missile
ject
in 2017
war-
6 MIRVs,
ed to hit
nt target
3rd stage
solid booster
ge
oster
12 metres tall
e solid
2.5
metres
wide

Now both India and Pakistan have the assured capability of destroying each other – Mutaual Assured Destruction has come to South Asia. This is the reason that it becomes imperative for both nations to amicably address their issues and attempt to resolve it, before any hawkish government from either side decides to start thinking of the unthinkable – nuclear war. The current fundamentalist Indian BJP government of Prime Minister modie and its backing from groups such as the RSS (Indian Fascists whose views are similar to Nazi Germany of the past) – could use heavy handed tactics in Indian security issues and attempt to blame the Pakistani government for their failures (possible false flag operations) could lead to a horendous nuclear war within the subcontinent and this will have global ramifications.

Pakistan Navy Khalid Class (Agosta) submarine on patrol

Indian aircraft carrier with Mig-29 Fulcrum multi-role combat aircraft[49]

---

[49] India eyes military expansion; Sitharaman to spend Diwali with soldiers in Andaman tri-service command - http://www.civilsdaily.com/story/defence-sector/

Overall Nuclear delivery systems

A list of India's potential nuclear delivery vehicles is provided here. The
nuclear weapons potential of India's estimated fissile material stocks will be
equivalent to 130 warheads by the end of 2017.

India, Possible Nuclear Delivery Vehicles, 2018

AIRCRAFT				
Type-	Number Deployed	Range (Km)	Payload (Kg)	Speed
Jaguar	117	2,600	4,750	Mach 1.5
Mig-27	65	1,100	4,000	Mach 1.7
Mig-29	63	1,500	3,000	Mach 2.35
Su-30MKI	250	3,000	8,000	Mach 2.0
Mirage 2000	50	1,850	6,300	Mach 2.2

Land-Based Missiles				
Type-	Number Deployed	Range (Km)	Payload (Kg)	Classification
Prithvi-150	Operational	150	1,000	BSRBM

Prithvi-250	Operational	250	500	SRBM
Prithvi-350	Operational	350	500	SRBM
Agni 1	Operational	700	1,000	MRBM
Agni 2/3/4	Tested/Dev	2,500-4,000	1,000	IRBM
Agni 5	Tested/Dev	5,000-8,000	Unknown	ICBM

Submarine-Launched Ballistic Missiles

Type-	Number Deployed	Range (Km)	Payload (Kg)	Classification
Sagarika	Tested/Dev	700-750	500	SLBM
Shaurya	Tested/Dev	3,000-3,500	500	SLBM

Source: federation of American scientists, Centre for Defence Information, PIADS intelligence Unit[50]

---

[50] Centre for Defence Information (Internet)

India's Nuclear capable aircraft

Jaguar	**MIG-27 Flogger**

Jaguar is a dedicated attack/strike aircraft of the IAF

Mig-27 Flogger – primary attack aircraft in the IAF

MIG-29 Fulcrum	**Su-30MKI Flanker**

<table>
<tr><td>Mirage 2000

</td><td>LCA Tejas

</td></tr>
</table>

A list of Pakistan's potential nuclear delivery vehicles is provided here. The nuclear weapons potential of Pakistan's estimated fissile material stock is 140 warheads by the end of 2017.

Pakistan, Possible Nuclear Delivery Vehicles, 2018

AIRCRAFT				
<u>Type-</u>	Number Deployed	Range (Km)	Payload (Kg)	<u>Classification</u>
JF-17 Thunder	85	600	3,500	Mach 1.12
Mirage III/5	171	500	3,500	Mach 2.2
F-16	76	850	2,500	Mach 2

Land-Based Missiles				
Type-	Number Deployed	Range (Km)	Payload (Kg)	Classification
M-11	Storage (40-84)	280	800	SRBM
Hatf 9 Nasr	Operational	60-70	500	BSRBM
Hatf 1/A	Operational	70-100	500	BSRBM
Hatf 2 Abdali	Operational	180-200	500	SRBM
Hatf 3 Ghaznavi	Operational	290	500	SRBM
Shaheen 1/2	Operational	750-2,000	500	MRBM
Hatf 5 Ghauri	Operational	1,250-1,500	500-750	MRBM
Shaheen 3	Tested/Dev	2,750	Unknown	MRBM
Ababeel	Tesyted/Dev	2,200	Unknown	IRBM
	Operational	350-700	500	MRBM

Babur (GLCM)				
		Submarine Launched Cruise Missile (SLCM)		
Babur 3 (SLCM)	Tested/Dev	450-700	500	MRBM

Source: federation of American scientists, Centre for Defence Information, PIADS intelligence Unit[51]

CLASSIFICATIONS OF BALLISTIC MISSILES BY RANGE

BSRBM	Battlefield Range	Short	Upto 150km	Up to 94 miles
SRBM	Short Range		150-699km	94-499 miles
MRBM	Medium Range		700-2,499km	500-1,499 miles
IRBM	Intermediate Range		2,500-5,499km	1,500-3,437 miles
ICBM	Intercontinental		+5,000km	+3,438 miles
SLBM Range	Submarine Launched			No specific Classification

---

[51] Centre for Defence Information (Internet)

Pakistan's Nuclear capable aircraft

Pakistan's most sophisticated type – the US F-16 Falcon Multi-role combat aircraft

Pakistan Army Shaheen 3 nuclear capable ballistic missile

Pakistani Nuclear ballistic missile test

5 THE IMPACT OF A NUCLEAR WAR

Nuclear bombs are horendous weapons that have the ability of causing mass destruction. The bombs dropped on Japan by the USA in 1945 had compl;etely destroyed the Japanese cities of Horoshima and Nagasaki. The following were the casualty figures: Hiroshima – 135,000 Killed and Nagasaki – 50,000 Killed[52].

We will look into a potential modern conflict (Indo-Pakistan) that has the capacity to kill millions of people in a nuclear exchange. This is one of the reasons that these horific weapons need to be eliminated.

Disarming the countries with Nuclear Weapons

52

https://www.bbc.co.uk/history/ww2peopleswar/timeline/factfiles/nonflash/a6652262.shtml

The Impact of an Indo-Pakistan Nuclear War

India and Pakistan are estimated to have nuclear weapons between 130-150 nuclear warheads each. An analysis of the consequences of a nuclear war was undertaken by the Natural Resources defense Council (NRDC) on two given scenarios of using 10 Hiroshima-sized explosions without any fallout and 24 nuclear explosions with massive radioactive fallout. 15 kiloton yield (1 kiloton is equivalent to 1,000 tons of TNT) was the power on the bomb dropped on Hiroshima, Japan by the united states of America. For the purpose of this scenario, it is assumed that both India and Pakistan possess 15 kiloton yield of the Hiroshima weapon.[53]

Scenario 1: 10 Bombs on 10 South Asian Cities

Casualty data from the Hiroshima bomb to estimate what would happen if bombs exploded over 10 large South Asian cities was used: 5 in India and 5 in Pakistan. 10 nuclear weapons would kill 3 to 4 times more people per bomb than in Japan because of the higher urban densities in Indian and Pakistani cities. The 15-kiloton yield of the Hiroshima equivalent weapon was based on the following:[54]

- Deaths and severe injuries experienced at Hiroshima were mainly a function of how far people were from ground zero.
- Factors included whether people were in buildings or outdoors,
- The structural characteristics of the buildings themselves,
- The age and health of the victims at the time of the attack.
- The closer to ground zero, the higher fatality rate.
- Further away there were fewer fatalities and larger numbers of injuries.

---

[53] Syed Ali Abbas Zaidi's Blog, Consequences of India-Pakistan Nuclear War - https://plastictearz.wordpress.com/2010/02/09/consequences-of-india-pakistan-nuclear-war/

[54] Ibid

Estimated nuclear casualties for attacks on 10 large Indian and Pakistani cities

City Name	Total Population Within 5 Kilometers of Ground Zero	Number of Persons Killed	Number of Persons Severely Injured	Number of Persons Slightly Injured
India				
Bangalore	3,077,937	314,978	175,136	411,336
Bombay	3,143,284	477,713	228,648	476,633
Calcutta	3,520,344	357,202	198,218	466,336
Madras	3,252,628	364,291	196,226	448,948
New Delhi	1,638,744	176,518	94,231	217,853
Total India	14,632,937	1,690,702	892,459	2,021,106
Pakistan				
Faisalabad	2,376,478	336,239	174,351	373,967
Islamabad	798,583	154,067	66,744	129,935
Karachi	1,962,458	239,643	126,810	283,290
Lahore	2,682,092	258,139	149,649	354,095
Rawalpindi	1,589,828	183,791	96,846	220,585
Total Pakistan	9,409,439	1,171,879	614,400	1,361,872
India and Pakistan				
Total	24,042,376	2,862,581	1,506,859	3,382,978

Scenario 2: 24 Ground Bursts

In this scenario 24 nuclear explosions are detonated on the ground (unlike Hiroshima airburst, which resulted in great amounts of lethal radioactive fallout). It is assumed that a dozen 25 kiloton warheads would be detonated each in India and Pakistan. The results are as follows:[55]

---

[55] Syed Ali Abbas Zaidi's Blog, Consequences of India-Pakistan Nuclear War - https://plastictearz.wordpress.com/2010/02/09/consequences-of-india-pakistan-nuclear-war/

15 Indian and Pakistani cities attacked with 24 nuclear warheads

Country	City	City Population	Number of Attacking Bombs
Pakistan	Islamabad (national capital)	100-250 thousand	1
Pakistan	Karachi (provincial capital)	> 5 million	3
Pakistan	Lahore (provincial capital)	1-5 million	2
Pakistan	Peshawar (provincial capital)	0.5-1 million	1
Pakistan	Quetta (provincial capital)	250-500 thousand	1
Pakistan	Faisalabad	1-5 million	2
Pakistan	Hyderabad	0.5-1 million	1
Pakistan	Rawalpindi	0.5-1 million	1
India	New Dehli (national capital)	250-500 thousand	1
India	Bombay (provincial capital)	> 5 million	3
India	Delhi (provincial capital)	> 5 million	3
India	Jaipur (provincial capital)	1-5 million	2
India	Bhopal (provincial capital)	1-5 million	1
India	Ahmadabad	1-5 million	1
India	Pune	1-5 million	1

The NRDC results are as follows:

- 22.1 million people in India and Pakistan would be exposed to lethal radiation in the first two days after the attack.
- Another 8 million people would receive a severe radiation, causing severe radiation sickness and potentially death, especially for the very young, old or infirm.
- Approximately 30 million people would be threatened by the fallout from the attack, roughly divided between the two countries.
- Besides fallout, blast and fire would cause substantial destruction within roughly a mile-and-a-half of the bomb craters. NRDC estimates that 8.1 million people live within this radius of

destruction.[56]

According to another estimate (2013 research paper by the International Physicians for the Prevention of Nuclear War), 21 million people will be killed instantly with significant environmental damage on a global scale. It states, **"If India and Pakistan fought a war detonating 100 nuclear warheads (around half of their combined arsenal), each equivalent to a 15-kiloton Hiroshima bomb, more than 21 million people will be directly killed, about half the world's protective ozone layer would be destroyed, and a "nuclear winter" would cripple the monsoons and agriculture worldwide. An additional two billion people worldwide would face risks of severe starvation due to the climatic effects of the nuclear war"**.[57]

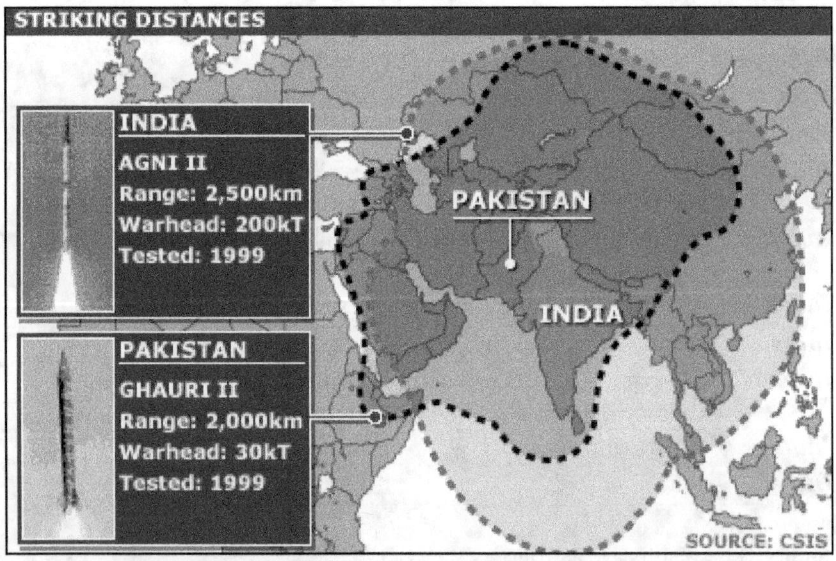

The above map is an estimate of the nuclear missile reach of both India and Pakistan

---

[56] Ibid

[57] Imagining the Unimaginable: India-Pakistan Nuclear Confrontation - https://thegeopolitics.com/imagining-the-unimaginable-india-pakistan-nuclear-confrontation/

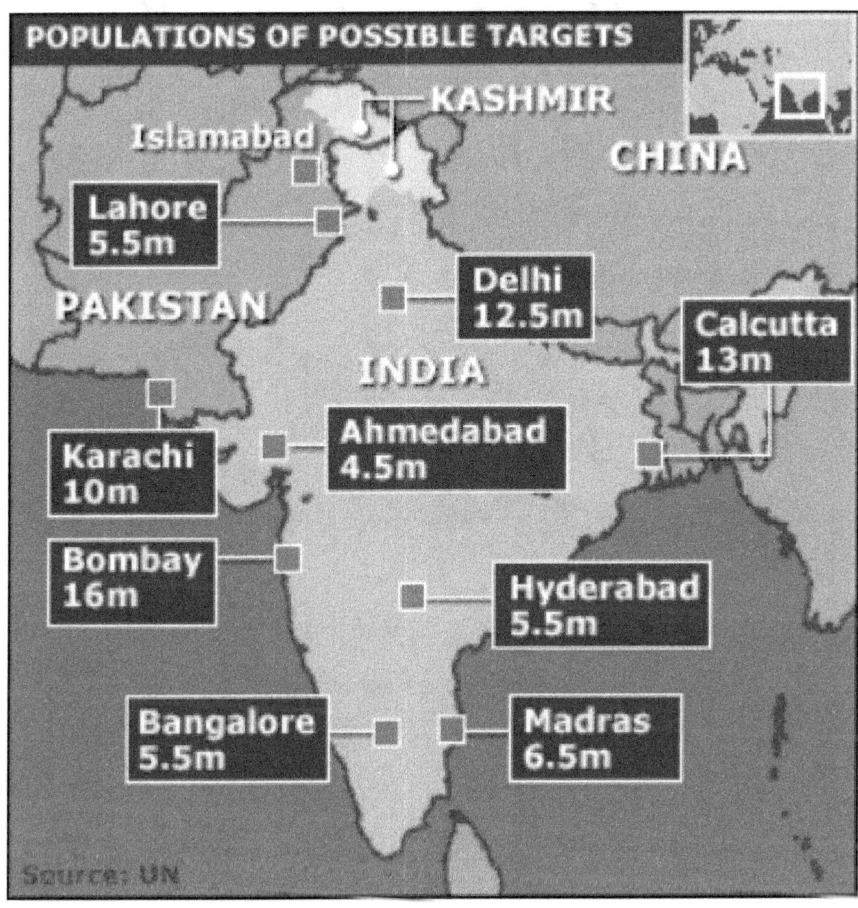

As can been seen that a nuclear exchange between India and Pakistan
would bring horrendous loss of lives with devastating environmental
consequences. A possible nuclear winter and the destruction of many lives
across the globe. In addition it would bring economic recession and
disruption of the global economic trade.[58]

---

[58] Ibid

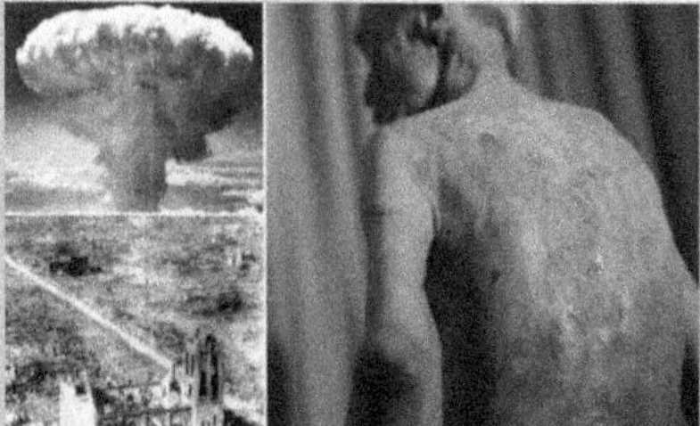

Horrific injuries due to a nuclear bomb (Hiroshima and Nagasaki - Japan)

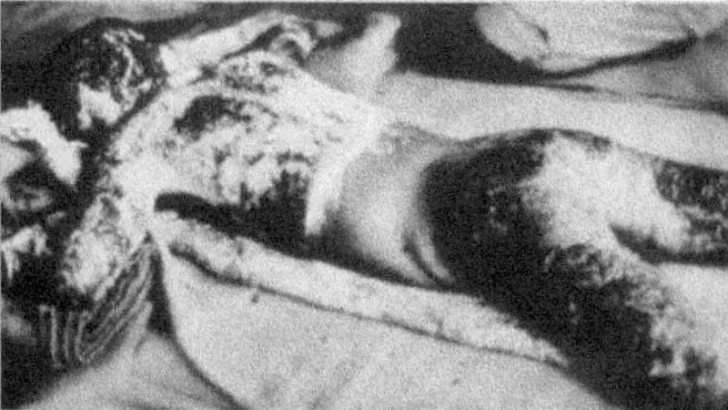

Horrific injuries caused by a nuclear bomb

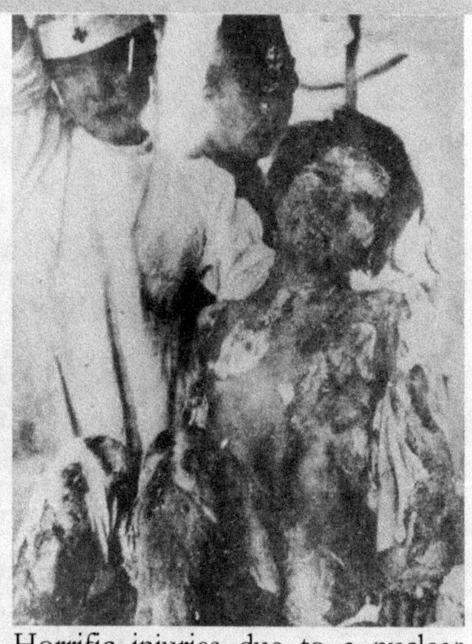

Horrific injuries due to a nuclear bomb (Hiroshima and Nagasaki - Japan)

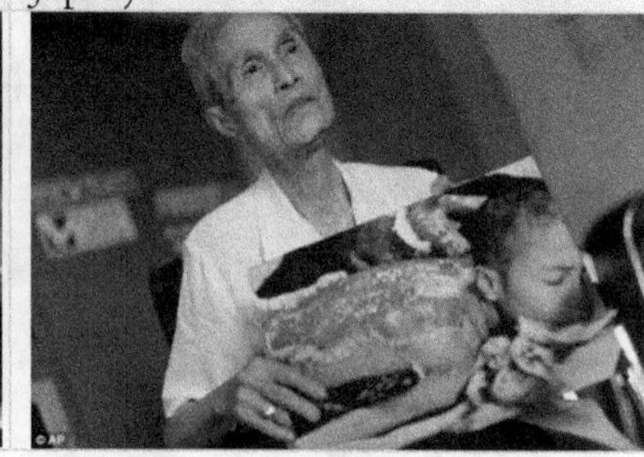

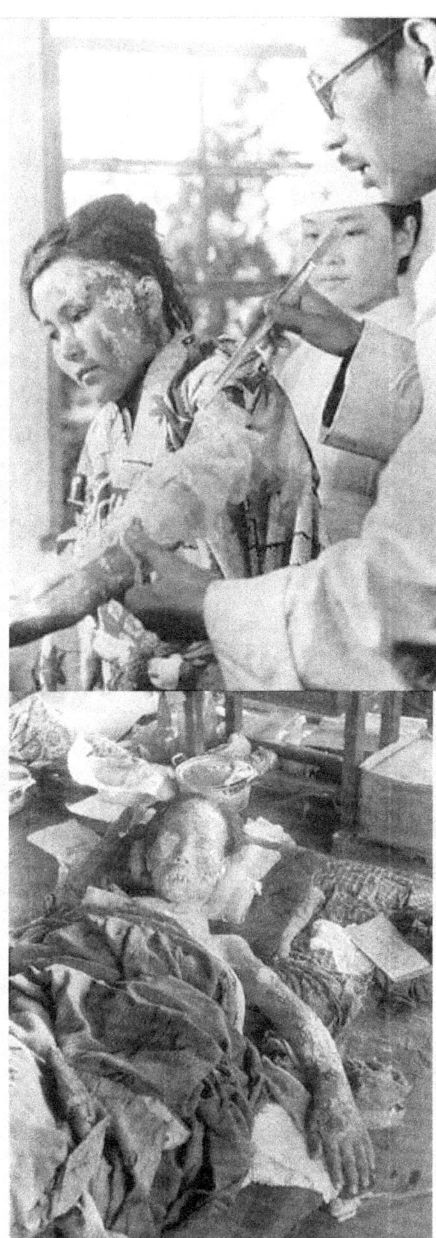

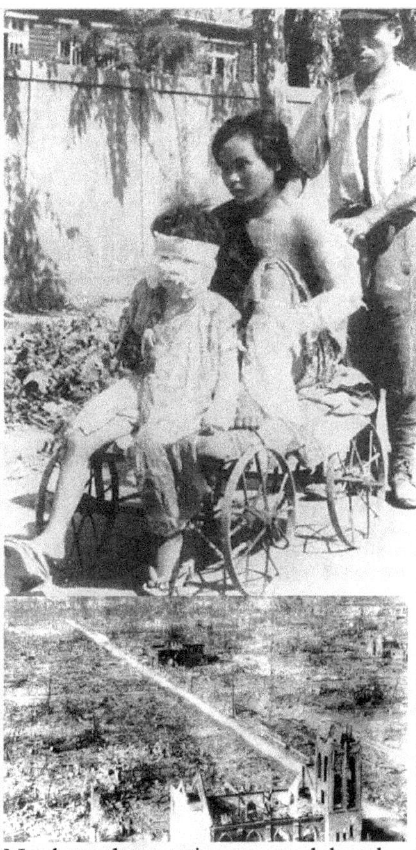

Nuclear devastation caused by the nuclear bombs dropped by the USA on Japan - Hiroshima and Nagasaki cities were destroyed with horendous injuries and casualties.

The impact on Indo-Pakistan nuclear war is unthinkable – but in reality it can easily be triggered by any miscalculation from either side. There are enough issues on the boil in this part of the world and it would not take too long for either side to misconstrue each other's intentions – which could lead to a nuclear holocaust.

India successfully test-fires nuclear capable Prithvi-II

Pakistani nuclear capable ballistic missile test

6 NUCLEAR DISARMAMENT

Arms Control and Confidence-Building Measures

The nuclear tests by a number of nations since 1945 have established a form of defence equilibrium. The consequences of a nuclear conflict would be enormously destructive, with neither side being a winner. There is a real concern that the long-standing hostility between various nuclear powers, such as the USA vs Russia, North Korea vs South Korea, China vs Taiwan, Israel Vs Iran, India vs Pakistan etc. could overwhelm any deterrent advantage gained from these nuclear weapons. The need for continued, relentless dialogue is all too apparent given the history of these nations.

Over the years a numerous bilateral nuclear arms control initiatives have been taken by the major global nuclear powers and also with regional powers, declaring, for example in the case of Pakistan, that it would be prepared to join the NPT or accept other non-proliferation measures if India did so. India has rejected these proposals, arguing that they do not address the nuclear threat India faces from China and that nuclear disarmament questions should be addressed as a global, rather than as a regional issue. Pakistan and India have, however adopted a number of bilateral confidence-building measures, including a military-to-military hotline and an agreement, which entered into force in January 1991, prohibiting the two states from attacking each other's nuclear installations. Lists of facilities covered by this agreement are now also exchanged periodically.[59]

Actual measures the nuclear powers could take

---

[59] Ashok Kapur, Pakistan's attitude to the NPT, Parchment Press, 1993, Pg25

Tackle any dispute Positively.

It is obvious that nuclear risk reduction will not get anywhere if there is no movement towards a broader settlement on any simmering border issues. Pending a solution to the dispute, progress is essential in dealing with the immediate sources of tension to build a climate of normalcy and pave the way to a just settlement.

Limitations placed on missile deployments and warheads.

Limitations on offensive weapon systems, curtailment of forward build-up of military cantonments and airfields would be a positive gesture for peace. None of these measures would deprive any of the nuclear powers of deterrence or defence capability.

Reduce the number of Soldiers and their main equipment deployed along the borders.

All nuclear powers with the agreement of all countries across the globe should focus on limitations on the number of troops, armoured and mechanised formations from each other's borders, eventually leading to the reduction of conventional offensive capabilities. That whole area can be declared a tank-free zone etc.

A reduction in new weapon systems.

A move towards prohibiting the induction of the latest technologies and weapons into their conventional forces would also be welcome. The underlying mutual minimal nuclear deterrence would lessen the need for the importance of 'state-of-the-art' weapons technologies. Defence acquisitions of new weapon systems and new technology should be made the subject of mutual discussions. For this reason, any nuclear risk reduction objective requires addressing the conventional asymmetry between the nuclear powers. These are already regarded as both feasible and cost-effective by each countries respective defence planners.

Increase nuclear co-operation between each other.

The eventual recognition and acceptance of each other's nuclear weapons capability can lead to co-operation, if desired, especially in terms of multilateral nuclear fuel centres, where technology can be jointly controlled. Given the problem all countries face in terms of conventional power generation, including the costs, nuclear power can become a viable alternative. Here the security route can eventually lead to direct economic benefits.[60]

Nuclear Powers should sign a Non-Aggression Pact.

All nuclear powers must move towards evolving a non-aggression pact –
either at the bilateral level or at the global nations multilateral level. Such a
pact differs from a no-war pact and does not deny the use of the military
option in self-defence – it only denies parties the option of aggressing
against other parties to the pact. It calls on both sides to commit to
agreements not to take aggressive measures against each other within a
military framework. A non-aggression pact will further build on the
confidence-and security-building measures (CSBMs) involving the hot-line,
communication facilities between commanders on all sides.[61]

Sign the major International Treaties.

Along with a proposal for a non-aggression pact, all nuclear powers with
the rest of countries across the world must go a step further in its moves
towards joining and agreeing to sign the **CTBT** as a nuclear weapon state.

The Comprehensive Test Ban Treaty (CTBT) - As for the CTBT itself, it deals
specifically with nuclear tests which it seeks to prohibit completely. Its
verification and on – site clauses also deal with test sites and not with
reactors and other weapons – producing installations.[62]

The Non-Proliferation Treaty (NPT) – All countries need to ensure that all sign
the NPT and ensure that the abolition of nuclear weapons.

Missile Technology Control Regime (MTCR) -. The MTCR is basically a suppliers
club and places no restrictions on member states developing their own
missile systems, but an agreement should be made to eliminate these
weapons as they will cause more pressures for the rival nation to acquire
one.[63]

Until such times as the conflicts are resolved at least, the global nations will
be refraining themselves from unrestrained and destabilising arms races -
and will have moved from a cold war style, unstable relationship to a more
stable, détente framework of interaction.

---

[60] Ibid

[61] Ibid

[62] Lodhi, op cit:12

[63] Ibid

The goal of international efforts should now progressively turn to preventing further nuclear tests, persuading all nations to halt the production of fissile materials for nuclear explosives and taking other steps to head off a nuclear Arms Race, such as pressing all sides to curb their ballistic missile programmes.

US President Barack Obama and other world leaders wave at the Nuclear Security Summit in 2016

In April 2016, approximately 130 countries said they were nearing agreement on a global non-proliferation pact - however 8 other states believed to have nuclear weapons did not support it. With the necessary political will the ban was achievable. However, the nuclear powers (USA, Russia, UK, France, China, India, Pakistan, North Korea and Israel) all refused to do this. Instead of adopting a total ban, the United States and other nuclear powers wanted to strengthen and reaffirm the nearly half-century-old Nuclear Non-proliferation Treaty. These double standards cannot be justified or maintained as it will encourage other states to eventually acquire the same technology, primarily to enhance their own security.[64]

---

[64] UN treaty to ban nuclear weapons may be adopted soon - https://www.timesofisrael.com/un-treaty-to-ban-nuclear-weapons-may-be-adopted-soon/

The NPT primary aim is to stop the spread of nuclear weapons away from the five original weapons powers — the US, Russia, Britain, France and China. It wants non-nuclear signatory nations not to pursue nuclear weapons in exchange for a promise by the five nuclear powers to move toward nuclear disarmament — and to promise non-nuclear states access to peaceful nuclear technology to produce nuclear power.[65] It has been many decades and the declared powers have not reduced or eradicated their nuclear weapons, on the contrary they are developing more powerful and sophisticated nuclear bombs.

Ballistic missile – Arms Control

Moreover, it was revealed how the nuclear expenditure and trade exacerbates conflict, promotes human rights abuses and worsens poverty in developing countries. The most obvious adverse impact of the nuclear arms trade on health is loss of life and maiming from the use of weapons in conflicts. Developed countries suffer damage to their health and human services when considerable resources are diverted to military expenditure. However, the relative impact of military expenditures and conflict on developing countries is much higher, and often catastrophic, by depriving a large portion of the population of essential food, shelter, medicine, economic opportunities and education.

---

[65] Ibid

Furthermore, the physical and psychological damage inflicted specifically on children is harmful – through loss of (or separation from) families, loss of education, destruction of homes, exposure to murder and other violence, sexual abuse, abduction, torture, slavery, and forcible conscription as soldiers.

The money used to buy conventional and nuclear arms can instead be used to solve the world problems. The amount of money the world spends on arms if used for humanitarian needs would wipe out all diseases/poverty and hunger in many countries in the world. The nuclear arms acquisition and development is in no doubt but immoral the desire for acquiring nuclear weapons cannot be morally justified.

CND Peace symbol[66]

A global ban on nuclear weapons can be achieved successfully in the future - if more public pressure is put on each countries respective political leadership then they will be encouraged to make a nuclear weapons ban effective. This ban would benefit nations by eliminating nuclear weapons and making them illegal in order to prevent them from being ever utilised. [67]

Conferences and negotiations should be commenced by the nation as a form of treaty to ban nuclear weapons. With committed nations, the remaining state who may not play a part in nuclear weapons may also consider negotiating with a nuclear ban taking place.   If this ban is not implemented, then alternatively the stratagem is to continue allowing the nuclear armed nations to control the process and sustain the two-tier systems and treaty regimes – this will not eradicate nuclear weapons.

---

[66] https://pixabay.com/en/peace-symbols-signs-black-white-24078/
[67] http://www.icanw.org/faqs-2/

There have been successful ban on weapons, such as the following:

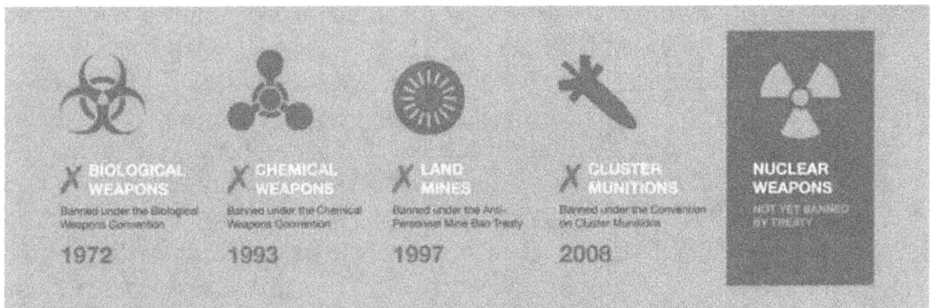

Where there is a will there is a way – abolition of nuclear weapons[68]

For instance, prohibiting biological and chemical weapons are good examples, where with determination a global treaty has been initiated which will eliminate these horrific weapons. Like the biological and chemical weapons treaties, a nuclear weapons ban would allow the nation to gain such supplies as long as they agree to eliminate the weapons within a set period of time. Hence, once nations have joined, further agreements could be formed and settled over time to ensure that the supply of weapons are destroyed in a certifiable and unalterable manner. South Africa is an excellent example of a country that has voluntary destroyed its nuclear bombs and signed the NPT treaty – it is a great examples of nuclear free zones.

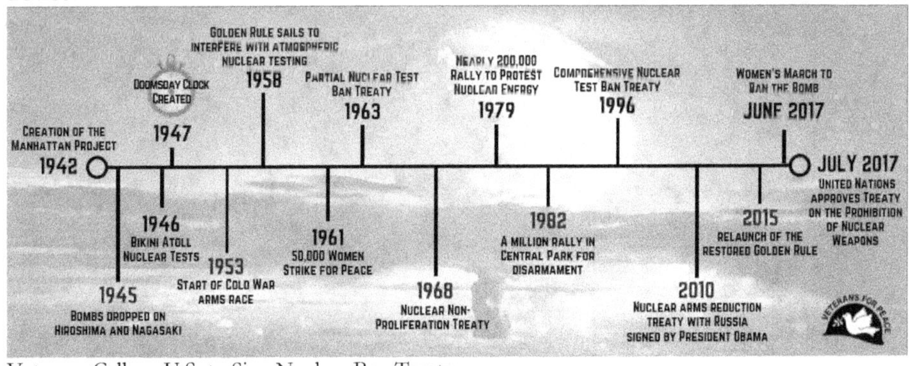

Veterans Call on U.S. to Sign Nuclear Ban Treaty

---

[68] http://www.icanw.org/faqs-2/

7 PEACE EDUCATION

The modern world has been prone to an increasing trend in destructive conflicts and wars that have devastated regions across the globe. Since the  First World War, there has been a rapid increase in the development of various methods to kill one another. The massive loss of lives and the human suffering (and also environmental degradation) has continued with an increase in lethality and fervour. Harris (2004) states, "During this past century there has been growth in social concerns about horrific forms of violence, like ecocide, genocide, modern warfare, ethnic hatred, racism, sexual abuse and domestic violence".

Many countries are currently been shaken by violent and intractable conflicts, including Iraq, Syria, Israel, Nigeria, Ukraine and Yemen. The list continues with a number of conflicts across the world that have the potential to cause huge loss of life. The conflict over the disputed territory of Kashmir between India and Pakistan has the potential to escalate to a nuclear level (as both countries possess nuclear weapons).

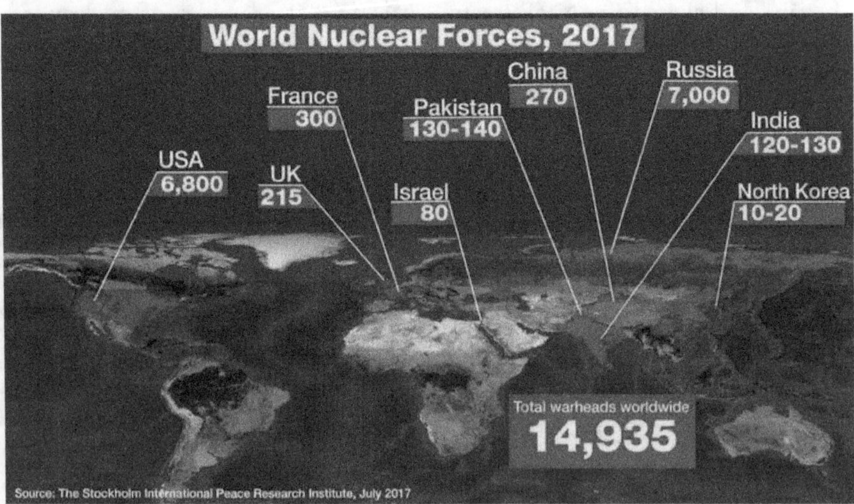

Harris (2004) further mentions that there is, "a corresponding growth in the field of peace education where educators, from early child care to adult, use their professional skills to warn fellow citizens about imminent dangers and advise them about paths to peace".

Culp (2017) argues that, "in the context of violent and intractable conflicts, peace education appears to be an effective instrument to promote peace because it holds the promise to empower future generations to solve many of those problems which present generations have had difficulty resolving". Culp further contends (2017), "Teaching people to interact with each other on peaceful terms is vital for social life of all groups – and even in the absence of any crisis".

Peace Studies does not have a clear agreed definition at this moment. Butt et al., (2011), noted, "Peace is a vague word. For some it means silence, calm and quiet, while other perceive it is an "end to quarrel", no conflict, no war, no violence, or no dispute (Mehmooda, 2006). According to Harris and Synott, Peace Education is a successions of 'teaching encounters' that draw from people:
1)   People's want for peace,
2)   Non-violent alternatives for dealing with conflict
3)   Skills for critical examination of structural measures that produce and legitimize injustice and equality (Harris and Synott, 2004).

Danesh (2006) argues that peace education is an elusive concept and has become more important due to the ever increasing trend of conflicts across the world. Accordingly, current peace education activities have been put under four categories:

Peace education 'mainly as a matter of changing mind-set', peace education 'mainly as a matter of cultivating a set of skills', peace education 'mainly a matter of promoting human rights, and finally, peace education as a 'matter of environmentalism, disarmament, and the promotion of a culture of peace' (Salomon, 2002). Moreover, ten goals for effective peace education had been identified by Harris (2002).

This shows that there has been widespread debate amongst the international community in regards to finding ways of increasing human security via the various processes of peace education.

Ellison (2014), noted the important study by Bush and Satarelli (2000) that had highlighted the "two faces of education and its role in both fuelling and mitigating conflict". In this study a number of examples were provided to show the ways in which education was used to intensify intergroup hostility. Such as the following:

(1) Education used as a weapon in cultural repression (the refusal to allow the Kurdish minority in Turkey to use their language in schools),
(2) Denial of education as a weapon of war (destruction of schools in Mozambique and the forced closure of Palestinian schools by Israel),
(3) Manipulation of textbooks (negative ethnic stereotypes in Rwanda and depiction of Tamils as the historic enemies of the Sinhalese in Sri Lanka).

Ellison (2014) also mentions the numerous studies that have discussed the many ways that the school system might reproduce social and gender inequalities that may be a catalyst for war (Davis, 2004).

Butt et al., (2011), noted, "Peace education is educating all people for peace to satisfy their physical and social needs through individual and group action at the micro (interpersonal) and macro (local, national, and global inter group) levels" (Yousaf et al., 2010). In addition, "The aim of peace education is to draw out, enrich, deepen and place in context students' thinking about the concept of peace" (Bretherton, et al., 2002)

The globalisation of the world and the regular tourism across it has led some to expand on the concept of peace. Ward (2009) has used the term 'peace tourism' in which he describes the term as, "self-initiated travel by an individual citizen to explore a (new) nation and its people using personal resources – time, financial, interpersonal, etc.". He believes that this concept is relevant to, "citizens of nations involved in war, genocide, drug or human trafficking, arms sales or any systematic armed violence against other nations".

Butt et al., (2011), also mentions "that internet, cd-rom, children's books, traditional folk stories, proverbs, art work and artefacts, and language teaching can be used as creative avenues to introduce peace education concepts, skills and attitudes, whether in or out of the school context" (Fountain, Susan, 1999).

The daily news of violent conflicts around the world and the trade in the buying and selling of weapons has increased human misery, poverty and loss of life. Peace education is a way of embedding positive methods to reduce the arms trade and ensure a more peaceful world.

Peace Education needs to become mandatory in all educational institutions and also should be a requirement for all government employees - confirms the positivity in this area and the desire to have this implemented in general education. Butt et al., (2011), further contends, "Peace education is most effective when the skills of peace and conflict resolution are learned actively and are modelled by the school environment in which pupils are taught" (Baldo and Furniss, 1998).

Peace Education can reform individuals positively. Butt et al., (2011), stated "Peace Education is currently considered to be both a philosophy and a process involving skill, including listening, reflection, problem solving, co-operation and conflict resolution. The process involves empowering people with the skills, attitude and knowledge to create a safe world and build a sustainable environment. The philosophy teaches nonviolence, love, compassion, and reverence for all life" (Harris and Morrison, 1988).

There is a high chance that peace education can reduce the acquisition and development of nuclear weapons. If more and more people are aware of the alternative methods of resolving conflicts and with individual mind-set changed positively towards a peaceful world. – then the menace of nuclear weapons trade can be curtailed. The nuclear arms race is the mechanism that fuels the simmering disputes and conflicts across the world.

North Korean Ballistic missile test of its nuclear capable missile

8 CONCLUSION

The acquisition and development of nuclear arms has had adverse consequences on many nations security. It does not do any good to the human race where millions of people are dying due to wars, poverty, hunger, lack of proper health facilities and environmental damage caused due to many reasons, mainly war.

The five declared nuclear weapon states are continuing an agreed system amongst themselves that is clearly based on apartheid and in addition have the veto power in United Nations Security council (UNSC), to maintain their monopoly of catastrophic destruction and blackmail.

North Korean Ballistic missiles on parade

It has been argued that, the 'nuclear weapons club' mirrors the world's political and racial divisions. This was in reference to a small group of nuclear powers who assumed that they had the rights to have these horrific weapons but other are not allowed to enter this 'special members' club.

The nuclear weapons states have had a considerable say on who is allowed to have nuclear weapons and who are not. They have consistently used bullying and arms-twisting tactics and have shown hypocrisy and double standards in order to maintain their nuclear hegemony.

NUCLEAR APARTHEID: BULLYING, HYPOCRISY, AND THE DOUBLE
STANDARDS ON NUCLEAR WEAPONS

The Nuclear weapons states (NWS) have succeeded in limiting the nations with nuke making capability to a few since NPT came into force in 1968 by allowing direct attacks , sabotage and sanctions While the treaty required that nations without nuclear weapons commit not to acquire them; those with them committed themselves to move toward their elimination. Everyone's right to develop peaceful nuclear energy was allowed. However, the five NWS have done little towards eliminating their nuclear arsenals. Instead they have improved upon the lethality of their nukes and delivery systems.

The nuclear arms race won't stop unless people will unite themselves and say strong 'NO' for the corruption. People need to realise that this problem must be solved, otherwise it will get only worst. If we will let it happen, we will fight for the countries or country which never cared about any human rights or better future. It never been our fight, it never been our war. People want to live peacefully and arms should be used only to make sure people are safe and secure. Nuclear Arms must be eradicated and the money should be invested in other needy areas. Instead of spending billions governments could use the money to raise economy and help pure countries. If money would be used wisely, we would face brighter future with new technologies, which would help us to invent and explore. Every regular person should care more about the issues which stays in the shadow.

The huge spending on developing and maintaining nuclear arms, has neglected other key areas. Less money is spent on resolving conflict, promoting human rights and this worsens poverty in many countries across the world. Developed countries suffer damage to their health and human services when considerable resources are diverted to military expenditure (nuclear). However, the relative impact of military expenditures and conflict on developing countries is much higher, and often catastrophic, by depriving a large portion of the population of essential food, shelter, medicine, economic opportunities and education. Furthermore, the physical and psychological damage inflicted specifically on children is harmful — through loss of (or separation from) families, loss of education, destruction of homes, exposure to murder and other violence, sexual abuse, abduction, torture, slavery, and forcible conscription as soldiers.

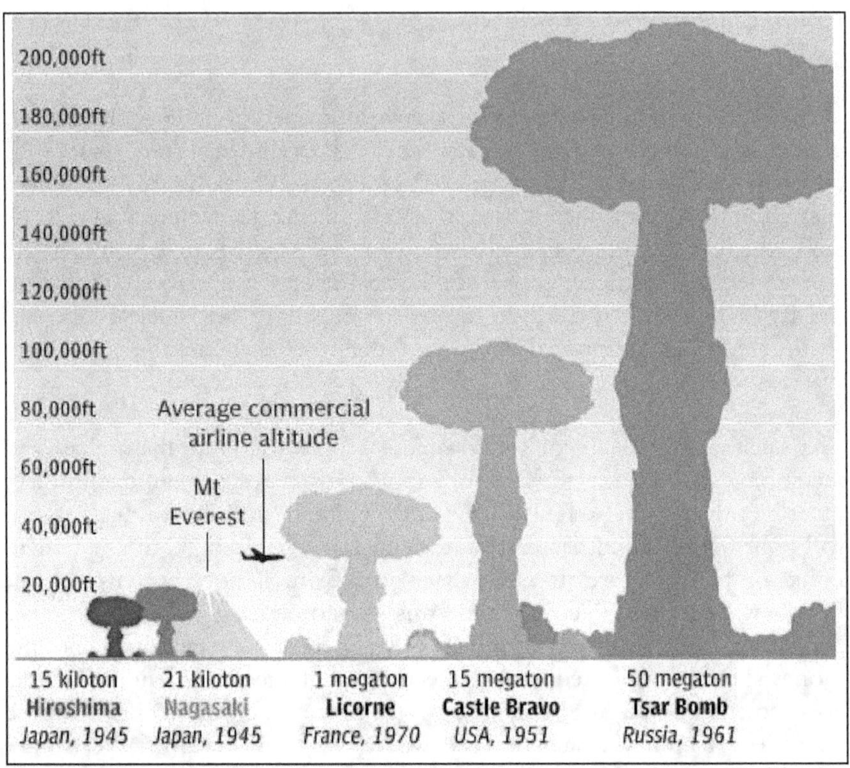

No matter the size of the nuclear weapons that have been made, the Non-Proliferation Treaty keeps all countries with nuclear weapons safe[69]

The money used to acquire and develop nuclear arms can instead be used to solve the world problems. The amount of money the world spends on military expenditure if used for humanitarian needs would wipe out all diseases/poverty and hunger in many countries in the world. The nuclear arms race is in no doubt but immoral the acquisition and trading of nuclear weapons and related techonologies cannot be morally justified.

To reiterate, Desmond Tutu (the Nobel peace laureate) stated, "that the world must not tolerate a system of nuclear apartheid in which it is considered legitimate for some states to possess nuclear arms but patently unacceptable for others to seek to acquire them". He argued, "that such a double standard has no basis for peace and security in the world. The

---

[69] https://history.libraries.wsu.edu/spring2017/2017/02/06/ra-2-russias-interest-in-nuclear-warfare-post-wwii/

Nuclear Non-Proliferation Treaty is not a license for the five original nuclear powers to cling to these weapons indefinitely".

South Africa is the only country so far that has relinquished its nuclear weapons and programme and destroyed its own nuclear bombs (estimated to have between 6-7 bombs) and has strongly advocated and adhered to the global NPT treaty and eventually the desire to have a Nuclear weapons free zone for the whole African continent. This is a model that could be applied to other continents (Goodson.2012).

Culp (2017) argues that, "in the context of violent and intractable conflicts, peace education appears to be an effective instrument to promote peace because it holds the promise to empower future generations to solve many of those problems which present generations have had difficulty resolving". Culp further contends (2017), "Teaching people to interact with each other on peaceful terms is vital for social life of all groups – and even in the absence of any crisis".

The former head of the International Atomic Energy Agency (IAEA), Mohamed El Baradei, described this two tier system as unworkable. He stated, "the way of thinking that it is morally reprehensible for some countries to pursue weapons of mass destruction yet morally acceptable for others to rely on them for security and indeed to continue to refine their capacities and postulate plans for their use" (Singh.2010). He argued that this two tier system would be difficult to work due to its discriminatory tendencies.

Over 2 billion people could be affected by a nuclear exchange in say India and Pakistan from only 50 nuclear bombs. Research had indicated this could have a tremendous effect on the environment and on food security. Hence, South Africa has shown a working model for nuclear disarmament that could be replicated across other regions. The NWS need to take action and lead from the front – this is the only viable way for complete global disarmament.

US B2 Stealth Nuclear capable bomber - Sustaining Nuclear Deterrence Requires New Capabilities

A U.S. Air Force B-2 Spirit Bomber and two F-15 Strike Eagle

References

Adams, J. (1992). Trading in Death – the Modern Arms Race, Pan Books Ltd.

Albright, David and Zamora, Tom. 1989. India and Pakistan go Nuclear. Washington. Bulletin of Atomic Scientists.

Albright, David. 1994. South Africa and the Affordable Bomb. The Bulletin of the Atomic Scientists.

Amnesty International - https://www.amnesty.org.uk/

Anna-Mart van Wyk.2012. Apartheid's bomb and regional liberation: Cold war perspectives. [Online]. Available at: http://www.freebookez.com/cold-war-and-african-liberation/

Arnett, Nuclear stability and arms sales to India, Arms Control Today, 1997

Ashok Kapur, Pakistan's attitude to the NPT, Parchment Press, 1993

B.H.Farmer, An Introduction to South Asia, Richard Clay & Co.Ltd, 1983

Babbage, Maria. 2008. White elephants: Why South Africa gave up the bomb and the implications for nuclear non-proliferation policy. [Online]. Available at: https://www.princeton.edu/jpia/past-issues-1/2004/11.pdf

Ben Dolven, Mark Manyin, Shirley Kan, Maritime Territorial Disputes in East Asia: Issues for Congress, CRS Report, 2014

Burrows, G. (2002). The No-Nonsense guide to the Arms Trade, New Internationalist Publications Ltd.

Butt, M. N., Iqbal, M., Ud-Din, M. N., Hussain, I., & Muhammad, N. (2011). Infuse concept of peace in curriculum development. Contemporary Issues in Education Research (CIER), 4(2), 27. doi:10.19030/cier.v4i2.4080
C. Philips, The nuclear Casebook, Polygon Books, 1983

Campaign Against Arms Trade (CAAT), Global Poverty, Online - https://www.caat.org.uk/issues/poverty
Carter , Jimmy. 2005. US is the main culprit in NPT failure. New Perspectives Quarterly 22 (3): 61-2.

Chapter Six: Asia, 2018, The Military Balance, vol. 118, no. 1, pp. 219

Christopher Walker and Michael Evans, Pakistan Feared Israeli Raid, The Times, Wednesday June 3, 1998

Christopher Walker, Israel's Helped India for 20 years, The Times, Thursday June 4, 1998

Cindy Shiner, International Herald Tribune, 1998

Cordesman, A.H. (1988). Armed Forces Journal, Western Strategic Interests and the India-Pakistan military balance, Ian Allan Ltd.

Culp, J. (2017). Against all odds: Peace education in times of crisis. Educational Philosophy and Theory, 49(10), 1029-1037. doi:10.1080/00131857.2016.1274954

Danesh, H. B. (2006). Towards an integrative theory of peace education. Journal of Peace Education, 3(1), 55-78. doi:10.1080/17400200500532151 David Albright and Tom Zamora, India and Pakistan go Nuclear, Bulletin of Atomic Scientists, 1989

Davis, Paul. 2009. Giving up the bomb: motivations and incentives. [Online]. Available at:
http://carleton.ca/npsia/wpcontent/uploads/davis_bomb.pdf

Dawn Weekly, Kashmir Policy, Touch Media Co.Ltd, 1998

Edward W. Desmond, Unity or Chaos?, Time, November 12, 1990

Eric Arnett, Military Capacity and the Risk of War-China, India, Pakistan and Iran, Oxford University Press, 1997

Erickson, J. L. (2015). Dangerous trade: Arms exports, human rights, and international reputation. New York: Columbia University Press.

Farmelo, Graham. 2012. *Nuclear apartheid, the international review.* [Online]. Available at:
http://www.tandfonline.com/doi/abs/10.1080/07075332.2012.667640#.U1UP_sJOWP8

Flickr - https://www.flickr.com/search/?text=jf-17%20thunder

Fraser, John. 2013. Abandoning Nuclear Weapons – Lessons from South Africa. [Online]. Available at:

http://www.ipsnews.net/2013/01/abandoning-nuclear-weapons-lessons-from-south-africa/

Freedman, L. (1985). Atlas of Global Strategy, MacMillan London Ltd.
Freedman, Lawrence. 2003. The Evolution of Nuclear Strategy. 3rd ed.
New York: Palgrave Macmillan.

Galtung, J. (1983). Peace education: Learning to hate war, love peace, and
to do something about it. International Review of Education /
Internationale Zeitschrift Für Erziehungswissenschaft / Revue
Internationale De l'Education, 29(3), 281-287. doi:10.1007/BF00597972
General Walter Walker, The Next Domino?, The Covenant Publishing
Co.Ltd, 1980

Gerson, Joseph. *Civil Society Statement to the UN High-Level Meeting on Nuclear
Disarmament.* [Online]. Available at: http://truth-out.org/author/itemlist/user/45734?limitstart=0

Goodson Donald. 2012. Catalytic Deterrence? Apartheid South Africa's
Nuclear Weapons Strategy. [Online]. Available at:
http://www.tandfonline.com/doi/pdf/10.1080/02589346.2012.683940#.U1JOD_FOWP8

Gross, Z. (2017). Revisiting peace education: Bridging theory and practice –
international and comparative perspectives – introduction. Research in
Comparative and International Education, 12(1), 3-8.
doi:10.1177/1745499917698290

Gusterson, Hugh. 2006. A Double Standard on Nuclear Weapons? MIT
Center for International Studies. [Online]. Available at:
http://web.mit.edu/cis/pdf/gusterson_audit.pdf

Hafeez Malik, Dilemmas of National Security and Co-operation, The
Macmillan Press Ltd, 1993

Harris, I. M. (2004). Peace education theory. Journal of Peace Education,
1(1), 5-20. doi:10.1080/1740020032000178276

Helen E. Purkitt and Stephen F. Burgess. 2002. South Africa's Nuclear
Decisions. [Online]. Available at:
http://www.mitpressjournals.org/doi/abs/10.1162/016228802320231271?journalCode=isec#.U1JRx_FOWP

India Today, India and Pakistan hours away from a nuclear war, 1994

India Today, India is now a nuclear weapon state, Living India Media Ltd, May 1998

India Today, India is now a Nuclear Weapon State, Living Media India Ltd, 1998

India Today, Pakistan's nuclear test, what now, June 1998

Indian Air Force - http://indianairforce.nic.in/

Indian Army - https://indianarmy.nic.in/index.aspx

Indian Navy - https://www.indiannavy.nic.in/

Inter Services Public Relations (ISPR) - https://www.ispr.gov.pk/

J. W. de Villiers, Roger Jardine, Mitchell Reiss. 1993. Why South Africa Gave Up the Bomb. [Online]. Available at: http://www.foreignaffairs.com/articles/49411/j-w-de-villiers-roger-jardine-mitchell-reiss/why-south-africa-gave-up-the-bomb

J.Goldstein & J. Pevehouse, International Relations, United States, 2007 Jane Nolan, Ballistic Missiles in the Third World, Brookings Institutions, 1991

Janes Defence Weekly (JDW), On the Line of Fire, Janes Information Group Ltd, 1998

Jo-Ansie van Wyka. 2012. Nuclear diplomacy as niche diplomacy: South Africa's post-apartheid relations with the International Atomic Energy Agency models and article dates explained. [Online]. Available at: http://www.tandfonline.com/doi/abs/10.1080/10220461.2012.706492#.U1UROcJOWP8

Kapur, S. Paul. 2007. Dangerous Deterrent: Nuclear Weapons Proliferation and Conflict in South Asia. Palo Alto, Calif, Stanford University Press.

Kazmi, Zahir. 2010. Neo-nuclear apartheid. [Online]. Available at: http://www.dawn.com/news/594849/neo-nuclear-apartheid

Lauritzen, S. M. (2016). Building peace through education in a post-conflict environment: A case study exploring perceptions of best practices. International Journal of Educational Development, 51, 77-83. doi:10.1016/j.ijedudev.2016.09.001

Lawrence Freedman, Atlas of Global Strategy, Macmillan Press Ltd, 1985

Liberman, Peter. 2008. Israel and the South African bomb. New York. The
Nonproliferation Review.

Mahnaz Ipahani, Pakistan: dimensions of insecurity, Brassey's, 1990

Michael Klare, East Asia's Militaries Muscle Up, The Bulletin of the Atomic
Scientists Publishers, 1997

Moore, J.D.L. 1987. South Africa and Nuclear Proliferation. London:
MacMillan Press.

Nils Bhinda, The Kashmir Conflict-1990, Earthscan Publication Ltd, 1994

Norris, Robert S. and Hans M. Kristensen. 2005. British Nuclear Forces,
2005. Bulletin of the Atomic Scientists.

Official Gateway To The Government Of Pakistan -
http://www.pakistan.gov.pk/index.html

Oxfam - https://www.oxfam.org/en/research/wealth-having-it-all-and-
wanting-more

Pakistan Air Force - http://www.paf.gov.pk/

Perkovich, George.2010. *The Obama Nuclear Agenda One Year After Prague.*
[Online]. Available at: http://carnegieendowment.org/files/prague41.pdf

Pixabay -
https://pixabay.com/en/photos/?q=military&image_type=&cat=&min_h
eight=&min_width=&order=popular&pagi=2

Powell Anita. 2014. South Africa Leads Continent in Nuclear Development.
[Online]. Available at: http://www.voanews.com/content/south-africa-
leads-africa-in-nuclear-development/1880246.html

Sean Kay, Global Security in the Twenty-First Century, Rowman &
Littlefield Publishers, Inc, 2006
Shane J. Maddock. 2010. Nuclear Apartheid: The Quest for American
Atomic Supremacy from World War II to the Present. Chapel Hill:
University of North Carolina Press.

Singh, Gajendra. 2010. Nuclear Armed Bullies and NPT Review Western nuclear powers, China and Pakistan are the Worst Proliferators. [Online]. Available at:
www.boloji.com/index.cfm?md=content&sd=articles&articleID=9339

Singh, Jaswant. 1998. Against Nuclear Apartheid. [Online]. Available at:
http://www.jstor.org/stable/20049049

SIPRI - https://www.sipri.org/

SIPRI Yearbook (2014) – Armaments, Disarmament and International Security, Oxford University Press Inc., New York.

Smith Ellison, C. (2014). The role of education in peacebuilding: An analysis of five change theories in sierra leone. Compare: A Journal of Comparative and International Education, 44(2), 186-207. doi:10.1080/03057925.2012.734138

Stavrianakis, A. (2010;2013;). Taking aim at the arms trade: NGOs, global civil society and the world military order. London;New York;: Zed Books.

Stephenson, C. M. (2012). Elise boulding and peace education: Theory, practice, and quaker faith. Journal of Peace Education, 9(2), 115-126. doi:10.1080/17400201.2012.700196

Tarock, Adam, 2006, Iran's Nuclear Programme and the West, Third World Quarterly, Vol. 27 (4), Routledge Taylor & Francis Ltd.

Tutu, Desmond. 2011. Ending Nuclear Apartheid. [Online]. Available at:
http://www.themoscowtimes.com/opinion/article/ending-nuclear-apartheid/440153.html

UNODA. 1999. Nuclear weapons free zones. [Online]. Available at:
http://www.un.org/disarmament/WMD/Nuclear/NWFZ.shtml

Van Wyk, J. -A. 2015. South africa's post-apartheid nuclear diplomacy: Practice and principles. Insight on Africa 7 (2): 108-19
Van Wyk, Jo-Ansie, and Anna-Mart van Wyk. 2015. From the nuclear laager to the non-proliferation club: South africa and the NPT.South African Historical Journal 67 (1): 32-46

Van Wyk, Jo-Ansie. 2012. Nuclear diplomacy as niche diplomacy: South africa's post-apartheid relations with the international atomic energy agency. South African Journal of International Affairs 19 (2): 179-200

Van Wyk, Jo-Ansie. 2012. Nuclear diplomacy as niche diplomacy: South Africa's post-apartheid relations with the International Atomic Energy Agency models and article dates explained. [Online]. Available at: http://www.tandfonline.com/doi/abs/10.1080/10220461.2012.706492#.U 1UROcJOWP8

Van Wyk, Jo-Ansie. 2014. Africa and the 2015 NPT review conference: Agent or bystander? African Security Review 23 (4): 381-94

Walters, Ronald W. 1987. South Africa and the Bomb: Responsibility and Deterrence. Lexington: D.C. Heath and Company.

Ward, V. (2009). Conflicts of interest: Plasticity of peace tourism and the 21st century nation. Perspectives on Global Development and Technology, 8(2-3), 414-426. doi:10.1163/156914909X423953

Wessells, M. (2005). Child soldiers, peace education, and postconflict reconstruction for peace. Theory into Practice, 44(4), 363-369. doi:10.1207/s15430421tip4404_10

WHO. (2017, September 15). World hunger again on the rise, driven by conflict and climate change, new UN report says. Retrieved July 19, 2018, from http://www.who.int/news-room/detail/15-09-2017-world-hunger-again-on-the-rise-driven-by-conflict-and-climate-change-new-un-report-says

Wilson, A. (1983). The Disarmer's Handbook of Military technology and organization, Penguin Books.

Images in this book fall under the following categories

(a) public domain (applicable to most official photos released by the military/maufacturers)

(b) free for commercial use

(c) used with explicit permission from the owner (applicable to all images from private websites)

(d) assumed to fall under (a) or (b) (applicable to images in printed media where no image owner is identified)

Index

Recently released books (2018)

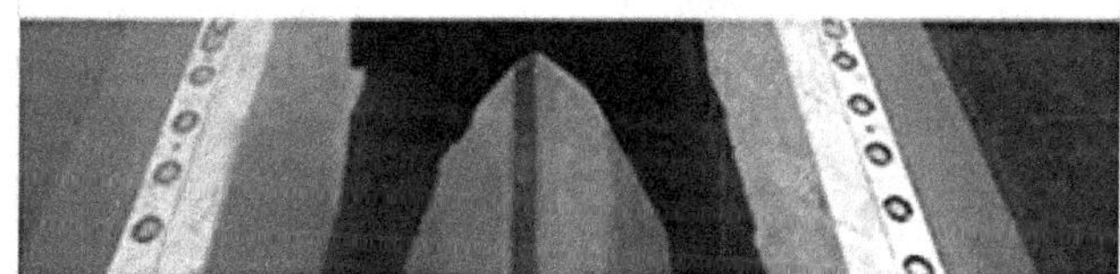

Major changes in East Asia have placed the region near the top of the World's strategic agenda. East Asia has until recently experienced the fastest regional economic growth rate in the world for many years. Economic co-operation has been flourishing and economic interests have become the major reason in reshaping East Asian international relations. However, there have also been changes in the security environment, due to many factors, such as the reduction of US forces in East Asia, the disintegration of the Soviet Union (the decline of the Soviet Union's presence in the region had led to renewed attention to traditional and potential rivalries among the major East Asian powers), and the concern of China's hegemonistic ambitions.

The astronomical rising costs of modern combat has resulted in many countries being deprived of purchasing a modern combat aircraft and this has had an adverse effect on their security. Many nations have tried to undertake cost-effective measures for their defence needs.

Countries can either purchase very expensive modern aircraft or buy older aircraft that can be expensive to operate due to their high maintenance requirements. The Pakistan Air Force had initiated the plan to co-develop an affordable modern multi-role fighter aircraft with China. Chengdu Aircraft Corporation (CAC) in collaboration with Pakistan Aeronautical Complex (PAC, Kamra) have jointly developed the JF-17 Thunder combat aircraft (also known as the FC-1 Xiaolong Fierce Dragon in China).

JF-17 Thunder is a sophisticated light-weight multi-role, all weather, day/night fighter aircraft that is manufactured by Pakistan and China. The JF-17 Thunder has become a very cost-effective aircraft that costs very little compared to other modern aircraft. Many countries have shown an interest and a few have started to make orders. Some have described the JF-17 as the 'Ultimate MiG-21' arguing that the Chinese/Pakistani JF-17 builds on a classic warplane – although it has no resemblance and its level of sophistication is comparable to current advanced fighter aircraft on the market. This very modern and capable aircraft has the potential to become a potent platform that can serve with numerous air forces across the world.

The global security challenges after the post-Cold war period has affected many countries. Pakistan's geography and location present its security planners with serious, almost irresolvable strategic and tactical problems. It borders the nuclear states of India and China, an ambitious Iran, and an unstable Afghanistan, which is perceived as a gateway to its commercial-strategic ambitions in Central Asia.

Pakistan's key security problems are a reflection of its history and domestic circumstances. The overriding concern of Pakistan is its internal and external security. Strategically, Pakistan lacks territorial depth. Its main cities and communication routes are relatively close to the border with India and are susceptible to attack. In addition, the headwaters of Pakistan's rivers and main irrigation systems originate from India. Pakistan's borders with India were also new and mainly unfortified and, in many places, were drawn in ways that made them indefensible. Because the borders were also un-demarcated, there was abundant chance for conflict. Pakistan has particularly been affected with a number of issues.

It has been argued by many that a Fourth generation/Hybrid war has been imposed on Pakistan, in order to break the nation (Balkanization of Pakistan into different parts) with the aim of making it either extremely weak or total destruction as a nation state (so that it is not able to challenge the hegemonistic ambitions of its adversaries).The purpose of this book is to assess the military security problems that Pakistan faces, and focus on its external security matters (military threats from neighbouring countries such as India, balance of power in the region, nuclear and ballistic missile threats, relationship with external powers, the high risk of war and its role on the 'War on Terror'), and its internal security problems (sectarianism, proliferation of small arms, refugees, ethnic violence, drug problem, economic weaknesses), and also its ability to cope with these problems.

MISCALCULATION: RISKS OF INADVERTENT NUCLEAR WAR

SAGHIR IQBAL

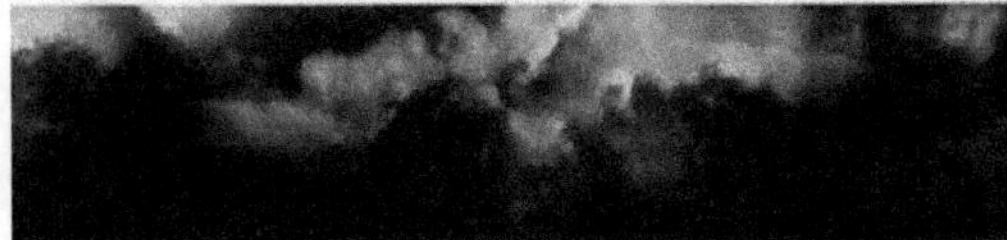

An impending nuclear holocaust is likely to happen, if the world community does not take action. A conflict that has been simmering for many years is beginning to spiral out of control. Two nuclear powers have an unresolved dispute that has increased tensions in the region.

Both countries are purchasing and developing sophisticated state-of-the-art weapons that could unleash great terror and destruction on the populations of both countries – with also serious global ramifications.

The world's most dangerous flashpoint, has the highest chance of a nuclear war occurring – it is deemed by many to be more serious that the Cuban Missile Crisis and North Korea's nuclear sabre rattling. The dispute needs to be amicably resolved between both nations and confidence building measures need to be implemented.

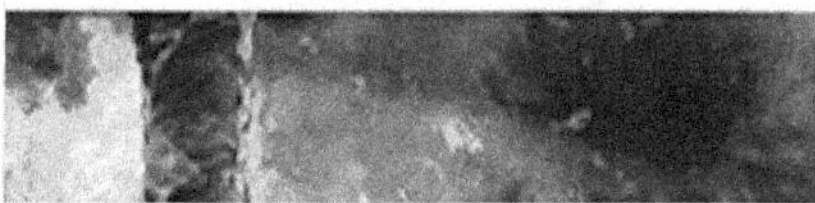

Pakistan faces a number of threats from internal and external forces – with the aim of weakening the country and an attempt to 'balkanise' Pakistan in to different parts. The Pakistani Chief of Army, General Qamar Javed Bajwa has said that "a hybrid war had been imposed on Pakistan to internally weaken it, but noted that the enemies were failing to divide the country on the basis of ethnicity and other identities".

Furthermore he states, "Our enemies know that they cannot beat us fair and square and have thus subjected us to a cruel, evil and protracted hybrid war. They are trying to weaken our resolve by weakening us from within". Conflicts in Ukraine, Israel and Lebanon (Hizbullah), Syria, Libya, War on Terror in Afghanistan and its impact in Pakistan etc., have resulted in multi-layered efforts to destabilise a functioning state and polarize its society. The centre of gravity is to target population in hybrid warfare. The aim of the adversary is to influence influential policy makers and key decision makers by combining kinetic operations with subversive efforts. The aggressor often resorts to covert actions, to avoid attribution or retribution. At the moment there is no universally accepted definition of hybrid wars – the term is too abstract and is seen by some as using a fancy term to refer to irregular methods to counter conventionally stronger forces.

Accordingly, many say that the new definitions of 4th generation or hybrid wars are really the repackaging of the traditional clash between the armed forces of nation states and the non-state insurgents. This book will be assessing Pakistan's insecurity and the hybrid wars imposed onto it by its adversaries. It will look at a number of issues that Pakistan is facing (military imbalance, economic and political weaknesses, internal and external security threats and the impact of hybrid warfare on Pakistan).

Each year billions of dollars' worth of arms are procured between various nations, despite the fact that many millions of people live in desperate poverty, many will die from hunger and hunger related diseases. Weapons of increasing firepower and the missiles to deliver them accurately are being acquired, mainly through the Global Arms Trade. This means that we must expect wars in the world to become increasingly violent and destructive.

This book focuses on what the arms trade is and its impact on the world, the wars which have resulted or were sustained by this trade. It is necessary to know which countries sell arms and which ones buy. Also it is important to have some idea of how large the trade is. The international trade in arms has considerably increased since World War 2. Major weapons (aircraft, missiles, tanks and ships) probably account for about one-half of the total trade in weapons and equipment. Many countries and their respective Military-Industrial Complex are 'making a killing' in the world's largest trade in the buying and selling of military technology (weapons).

NUCLEAR APARTHEID: BULLYING, HYPOCRISY, AND THE DOUBLE STANDARDS ON NUCLEAR WEAPONS

ABOUT THE AUTHOR

Saghir Iqbal is a researcher in International Relations and Security Studies. He is an experienced Intelligence Analyst and has achieved a number of qualifications in this field. He is also a Lecturer in Business Management as well as an Examiner for A Level History and Business. Saghir Iqbal has a subject specialism in the following areas:

International Politics of the Cold War 1945-1991
Conflict Resolution in International Society+
Global and North-South Security Studies
Britain in the World
Disarmament Processes: History and Theory
Nationalism and Ethnicity in Post-Cold War Politics
Middle East: Area in Conflict
European Security
International Politics of the Environment
The United Nations, Peacekeeping and Intervention
Disarmament Processes: Current Problems
Globalisation and the South
International Terrorism
International Politics and Security Studies
Introduction to Peace Studies
Politics of the Global Environment
Regional Security in East Asia
Critical Security studies

Recently released books (2018)

- Dangerous Flashpoints in East Asia: The Military Build-up
- JF-17 Thunder: The Making of a Modern Cost- effective Multi-role Combat Aircraft
- Pakistan's War Machine: An Encyclopedia of its Weapons, Strategy and Military Security
- Miscalculation: Risks of Inadvertent Nuclear War
- Hybrid Warfare and its Impact on Pakistan's Security
- Making a Killing: The Scourge of the Global Arms Trade

Website: www.saghir.co.uk

9 781983 910418